We Dared to Live

Live

A Tale of Courage and Survival

Based on the Memoir of Abrashe Szabrinski

Joe Sabrin

with *Chris Moore*

Translated from the Yiddish by Yeshaya Metal

gefen גפן
publishing house בית הוצאה לאור
JERUSALEM ● NEW YORK   Est. 1981

Copyright © Joe Sabrin
Jerusalem 2015/5775

All rights reserved. No part of this publication may be translated, reproduced, stored in a retrieval system or transmitted, in any form or by any means, electronic, mechanical, photocopying, recording or otherwise, without express written permission from the publishers.

Cover Design: Talya Shachar Albocher
Typesetting: Renana Typesetting

ISBN: 978-965-229-743-3

1 3 5 7 9 8 6 4 2

Gefen Publishing House Ltd.
6 Hatzvi Street
Jerusalem 94386, Israel
972-2-538-0247
orders@gefenpublishing.com

Gefen Books
11 Edison Place
Springfield, NJ 07081
516-593-1234
orders@gefenpublishing.com

www.gefenpublishing.com

Printed in Israel

Send for our free catalog

LIBRARY OF CONGRESS CATALOGING-IN-PUBLICATION DATA
Szabrinski, Abrashe, 1914–2001.
  We dared to live : a tale of courage and survival based on the memoir of Abrashe Szabrinski / [compiled and edited by] Joe Sabrin with Chris Moore ; translated from the Yiddish by Yeshaya Metal.
    pages cm
  Based on four previously unpublished manuscripts originally written
in Yiddish by Abrashe Szabrinski (Abraham Sabrin).
  ISBN 978-965-229-743-3
  1. Szabrinski, Abrashe, 1914–2001. 2. World War, 1939–1945 – Underground movements – Lithuania – Vilnius Region 3. Guerrilla warfare – Lithuania – Vilnius Region – History – 20th century. 4. Government, Resistance to – Lithuania – Vilnius Region – History – 20th century. 5. World War, 1939–1945 – Personal narratives, Jewish. 6. Jews – Lithuania – Vilnius Region – Biography. 7. Jewish soldiers – Lithuania – Vilnius Region – Biography. 8. Guerrillas – Lithuania – Vilnius Region – Biography. 9. Vilnius Region (Lithuania) – History, Military – 20th century. 10. Holocaust survivors--Biography. I. Sabrin, Joe, 1942– II. Moore, Chris, 1979– III. Title.
D802.L52V5564 2015
940.53'18092--dc23
[B]

2015019310

PARTISAN GROUPS AND NAZI STRONGHOLDS IN SOUTHERN POLAND, 1942–1945

Contents

Foreword by Abraham H. Foxman vii

Foreword by Claudia Moscovici ix

Editor's Note xiii

My Dad's Attaché Case. xvii

Acknowledgments. xix

Introduction by Abrashe Szabrinski. xxi

Chapter 1. 1

Chapter 2 11

Chapter 3 19

Chapter 4 25

Chapter 5 31

Chapter 6 41

Chapter 7 49

Chapter 8 59

Chapter 9 73

Chapter 10 89

Appendix 97

Notes 113

Foreword by Abraham H. Foxman

Abrashe Szabrinski's memoir of life on the run and with the partisans in WWII Poland and Lithuania is an engrossing saga that adds significantly to the body of Holocaust literature.

This story has particular interest for me because part of it takes place in Baranovich, where I was born in 1940. Szabrinski's description of what happened in that town when the Nazis took over reminds me once again of how fortunate I was that my Polish nanny took me in and raised me as a Christian child, while around me, all hell was happening for Jews.

This is a story that embodies all the conflicting emotions surrounding the Holocaust. It is, of course, about the systematic atrocities committed by the Nazis. In this case, we see them in a number of cities and towns where our protagonist appears. It is a story of great courage and great cowardice: Jews joining the partisans and bravely taking on the German war machine, and tales of betrayal where Jews are turned over to the Nazis.

It is a story of the highest moral values even under the worst of circumstances. And it is also about how the brutality of the conflict led to brutal violence in response. Most of all, Szabrinski's memoir is a moral tale of the consequences of powerlessness in the face of evil, and how people can regain their lives and their sense of who they are when they have the power to protect themselves.

This is the ultimate lesson for the Jewish people in the post-Holocaust world. Szabrinski's life conveys this message in a powerful and personal way.

Abraham H. Foxman, National Director,
Anti-Defamation League, August 2014

Foreword by Claudia Moscovici

On September 23, 2001, a few weeks after his granddaughter's wedding, Joe Sabrin's father, Abrashe Szabrinski, passed away. He was one of the few Holocaust survivors of Vilna (Vilnius). While Joe was going through his dad's belongings, he discovered an attaché case. It contained a war memoir written in Yiddish, a language he didn't understand. Filled with curiosity about his father's Holocaust experiences, which Abrashe rarely discussed with his family, Joe had it translated into English by the YIVO Institute for Jewish Research. Once he was able to read his father's memoir, Joe discovered an incredible tale of survival and courage. Abrashe Szabrinski "came to Vilna in July 1943 and by September 1943 was crawling through the sewers with eighty members of the FPO [*Fareynegte Partizaner Organizatsye* (United Partisan Organization)] on the day of the ghetto's liquidation. They were headed for the forest where this band of Jews would go on to fight together with the Russians. Despite the ever-present anti-Semitism, they fought on, and Joe's father, known by the code name 'Razel' was with them." A few of those who, like Abrashe Szabrinski, joined the Jewish partisan movement in the fight against the Nazis – destroying train tracks and railway cars, attacking SS convoys and guards in and around the Rudnicki Forest – managed to survive.

It is important to put this remarkable memoir in historical context. Vilna was a predominantly Jewish and Lithuanian city that Stalin had transferred back from Poland to Lithuania when he invaded Poland in September 1939. Nearly a quarter of a million Jews lived in Lithuania, including the newly acquired city of Vilna. During the German invasion in June 1941, many Lithuanian deserters joined the pro-fascist Lithuanian National Front and helped the Nazi Sonderkommando units (Einsatzgruppe A death squads) round up and shoot the Jews in the area. Under the German occupation, the Lithuanian government attempted to recapture Vilna and "nationalize" it. During the Nazi era, this meant an "ethnic cleansing" of about 60,000 Jews who lived in the area. Even before the establishment of the Vilna ghetto, the Nazis and their Lithuanian collaborators captured and murdered over 20,000 victims. Afterwards, the chances of escaping the ghetto alive were almost nonexistent.*

Between September 6, 1941, when the Vilna ghetto was forcibly established by the Nazis, and September 24, 1943, when it was liquidated, the Jews of Vilna lived under extremely difficult conditions, similar to what the inhabitants of the Lodz and Warsaw ghettos endured. They suffered from overcrowding, disease, starvation, forced labor, and the constant fear of mass deportations to concentration and death camps in the east, as well as shootings and beatings by the Nazis and local Lithuanian collaborators. The Nazis organized the ghetto to better control the victims and facilitate the plan for their ultimate extermination. They divided the ghetto into two parts, separated by a corridor of streets, which they patrolled along with the Lithuanians. The "small ghetto" was made up mostly of the elderly, women, children, and those deemed incapable of work. The "large ghetto" included the Jewish leadership as well as many able-bodied men and women who the Nazis could exploit for slave labor. First they murdered the inhabitants of the small ghetto, who they perceived as less useful. About 20,000 Jews remained in the larger community until September 1943, when Bruno Kitell, acting on orders from Heinrich Himmler, liquidated Vilna's ghetto.

Only a handful of young people survived; they included about 250 Jews employed as slave laborers in a German military vehicle plant, and those who joined the resistance movements and went into hiding in nearby forests to fight along with the partisans. Abrashe Szabrinski, who would become one of the leaders of the Jewish resistance in the area, was one of these few survivors. As he writes in the introduction to his memoir, "These Jews in Vilna were ready to fight to their last breath, as did the Jews of Warsaw. On the last day of Vilna's existence, the fighters were poised for war.... But rather than take on the Germans inside the ghetto and face immediate annihilation, orders were given to escape into the forest by means of the city's canals. There they could fight on."

Unlike the Warsaw ghetto, where the struggle was mainly a last-ditch effort at the end, when all hope for survival had been lost, resistance in the Vilna ghetto began early on, under the leadership of Isaac Wittenberg, Joseph Glazman, and Abba Kovner (the leaders of the FPO, which was formed in

* See Raul Hilberg, *Perpetrators Victims Bystanders* (New York: HarperCollins, 1992), pp. 98–99.

January 1942). Kovner, who would become a famous Israeli poet, urged Vilna's Jews to support the resistance. "We will not go like sheep to the slaughter" was his motto. The FPO opposed the attitude of appeasement adopted by Jacob Gens, the Judenrat and Jewish police leader, who opted for cooperating with the Nazis and their regular deportations in the hope of saving the Jewish leadership, their families, and those deemed capable of work. Gens viewed Jewish resistance as a dangerous provocation against the Germans and feared that the resistance movement would spread panic among the remaining inhabitants of the ghetto. In contrast, Kovner, Wittenberg, Szabrinski, and other members of the resistance maintained that the Jews couldn't trust the Nazis, and realized early on that the Germans' ultimate plan was to exterminate the Jewish people, not just exploit them as slave laborers.

When the Gestapo told Jacob Gens to hand over Isaac Wittenberg or else they would raze the ghetto to the ground and kill everyone in it, Wittenberg, at Gens's request, turned himself in. But he took a poison pill rather than allow himself to be tortured and killed by the Gestapo. Despite his acquiescence, the Gestapo summoned Gens to their headquarters on September 14, 1943, and shot him, suspecting him of collaborating with the resistance movement he had tried so hard to restrain. Shortly thereafter, the Nazis liquidated the entire ghetto despite their earlier reassurances to the Jewish council.

Abrashe Szabrinski's memoir, *We Dared to Live*, fills in details about the slaughter of Vilna's Jews by the Nazis, and describes the heroic and risky operations of the Jewish resistance and its sometimes uneasy alliance with the communist partisans. Along with a handful of other members of the resistance, Abrashe Szabrinski managed to survive the Holocaust and helped free Vilna from Nazi occupation. Yet, this was a bittersweet victory for the Jewish partisans. When they finally joined with the Russian army and took the city, they found it totally devoid of Jews. "Jerusalem of Lithuania" had been wiped off the face of the earth. We can find some solace in the fact that – thanks to this and other memoirs – at least its memory survives.

Claudia Moscovici, October 2014

This foreword will be part of *Holocaust Memory*, a forthcoming book of reviews of Holocaust memoirs, novels, and films being compiled by Claudia Moscovici, a writer (fiction and nonfiction), and university lecturer.

Editor's Note

I began the process of editing Abrashe Szabrinski's work with four separate and distinct manuscripts. These were English translations of his original Yiddish manuscripts. Of the four, Abrashe wrote one in traditional memoir format, in under thirty thousand words, beginning with an introduction and proceeding from there to tell his story in a more or less lineal progression until the end of the war. The other three manuscripts consisted of short anecdotes and stories punctuated here and there by longer narratives, totaling about seventeen thousand more words and containing little overall structure save for the association of the stories and the persons in them.

I then took the anecdotes and stories from the shorter manuscripts and wove them into the long memoir. The finished product came to form the document you now have before you. Often parts of the shorter stories exactly duplicated information from the longer version, while others fleshed out details and focused on personalities left out of the other accounts. I retained everything that was not duplicated, and worked to integrate the material as seamlessly as possible. There is only one instance where I left out an anecdote entirely in the edited manuscript because it seemed to function better as a note. It regards Yurgis and the destruction of Koniuchy, and can be found in "Military Punishments: Koniuchy," in chapter 9.

The main goal of the notes was to make the memoir accessible to the general reading public, and especially to younger readers who may be encountering this material for the first time. This is not to say that someone well read in the history of eastern Europe during WWII can't gain anything from this information; they can. Though some of the textboxes may seem self-explanatory, others will not.

While it is to Mr. Szabrinski's credit that he moves through his narrative with an eye to brevity, he often discusses people, places, and events that are historically, and from an American perspective, obscure and need to be defined because they are central to understanding, or more fully understanding, his narrative. Placing the notations right beside the text they pertain to allows the reader to see a fuller picture of the world that Mr. Szabrinski traveled through without having to flip back to an appendix or conduct research outside the book.

The notes also reference Abrashe's interview at Yad Vashem after the war. This interview can be found in the appendix.

The extent to which this book adds to the body of Holocaust literature is entirely due to Abrashe Szabrinski and the truly remarkable life he lived. I am grateful that he sat and wrote his memories. I am also thankful that his son Joe Sabrin, himself a Holocaust survivor, who as a baby was placed inside a Vilna orphanage for the duration of the war, found his father's writings and saw fit to contact me to prepare them for publication. I have certainly gained from studying the memoir and the period.

In the course of doing research for the work, I ordered many books. Among those I purchased was a used copy of *A Secret Press in Nazi Europe* by Isaac Kowalski. When the book arrived in my mailbox, I was surprised to learn that Abrashe had once owned this volume, as his name and address were indelibly stamped on the inside front cover.

I took this as a sign that I was on the right track to finding Abrashe in history, which I did. He was often named outright, in various spellings. Or, if he was not named, he provided a similar account to that of another survivor, as is the case with the story of Manye, which was also recalled by Dr. Zelik Levinbook (retold here in "Some Incidents That Occurred during the *Aktion*," chapter 2). Survivors such as Joseph Harmatz also recalled him to me in phone interviews.

Abrashe's memoir cuts a wide path through Polish, Lithuanian, Byelorussian, and Russian WWII history. It offers a unique and heroic perspective on well-known events, as well as a rare view of little-known episodes that should be brought to light, if only for the fact that most of the people who witnessed them were murdered.

And this gets to the heart of Abrashe's story: he survived when nearly everyone else died. In no small degree, his story reflects that of eastern European Jewry at this time. According to Lucy Dawidowicz, 90 percent of Polish and

Baltic Jews were murdered during the Holocaust. But again and again, Abrashe found himself part of the 10 percent who lived.* In his memoir he tells us how.

Chris Moore
March 31, 2015
Putnam County, New York

---

* Lucy S. Dawidowicz, *The War Against the Jews, 1933–45* (New York: Bantam Books, 1986), p. 403.

My Dad's Attaché Case

My dad died on September 23, 2001, exactly four weeks after my daughter's wedding. He had lived a full life. I think he had had enough. He went into the hospital though nothing in particular was wrong with him, and died. I was the last person to see him.

While we were sitting shivah for him, I went into his office. As I looked at his books, Isaac Kowalski's *A Secret Press in Nazi Europe* caught my eye. Kowalski was one of my father's friends and a fellow survivor. Then I turned and saw the Smith Corona Yiddish typewriter I had bought Dad years before. I had asked him again and again to let me see the pages of the memoir he was writing with it, but he wouldn't let them leave his room in Sayerville, New Jersey.

Now that I was in the room, I ventured toward his closet. That was where I found his brown attaché case. He took it with him everywhere: to the lawyers, the accountants. Taking the attaché case back to the desk, I opened it immediately and found the memoir I had heard so much about. The Yiddish made it look like a sacred text, like an artifact from a long-lost time. These were his last words. I slipped the pages into my jacket, knowing my mother would never let me leave with his memoir.

But I couldn't read it. At least not yet. Right then and there I began searching for a translator. I contacted the YIVO Institute and arranged for one. Within a few months I had the English before me. I was eager to see what he had written, but I could never have guessed what he had done. He and Mom had been closemouthed about what happened to them, to say the least. I knew they had been in Vilna, and that they had managed to get out; that I was born in the war, and that afterwards we moved to Turkheim, Germany, and then on to the United States.

What my father had really done during the war though was never discussed. I never knew about his time in Baranovich. I never knew of his time in the

Nazi labor camps. I never knew that he escaped from the Bezdani peat-digging camp on the day of its liquidation, and that of all places, he fled into the Vilna ghetto because he knew that with such a large ghetto population, the people there would have a connection with the partisans. Before all this, he, a Jew, had served as an officer in the Polish army. When Poland fell, he was recruited into the Soviet army. In other words, he knew how to handle a gun and he knew how to handle a group of fighting men, and he also knew that this would get him into the partisans.

He came to Vilna in July 1943 and by September was crawling through the sewers with eighty other members of the FPO (United Partisan Organization) on the day of the ghetto's liquidation. They were headed for the forest where this band of Jews would go on to fight together with the Russians. Despite the ever-present anti-Semitism, they fought on, and my father, known by the code name "Razel," with them. Then he became a commander, first of a unit named "Death to Fascists," and then, when the Jewish leadership was removed, as the commander of the Second, and almost exclusively Jewish unit, known as "For Victory." These Jewish partisans fought tooth and nail to help destroy the Nazi invaders. They destroyed train tracks, railway cars, and telegraph connections. They attacked convoys and guard posts. In the end, my father was with the partisans on the day they retook Vilna alongside the Red Army. A bittersweet victory since there were almost no Jews left at all. The Nazis were gone, but the "Jerusalem of Lithuania," as Vilna had been known, was gone forever.

In his book, *The Jewish Resistance*, partisan hero Chaim Lazar includes a brief list of those he calls "the best Jewish fighters in the partisan units in the forest of Rudnicki." He notes that "each one of them had a story both dramatic and unique." Chaim goes on to name my father, Abrashe Szabrinski, as one of those fighters. What follows is Abrashe's "dramatic and unique" story of those years.

Joe Sabrin
New York City, 2015

Acknowledgments

The publication of my father's memoir has been a labor of love for me and for my family. So first of all I would like to thank my wife of forty-six years, Sandy Sabrin (Born Sandra Hochstein, changed to Stone in America), and my children, Marcie Sabrin Berson and Yury Berson (and my grandson Alexy Berson) and Benjamin Paul Sabrin and Madeline Sabrin (and my granddaughters Nicolette and Meadow Eva). My wife and children loved Abrashe, and they and their extended families encouraged me to move forward with this project.

I wish to thank Yeshaya Metal of the YIVO Institute, who translated the memoir from the Yiddish.

I would also like to express my appreciation to all my friends who have supported me in the process of bringing my father's war memoir to publication. I would like to mention in particular Eric M. Lerner, who has been very supportive, making recommendations that were extremely helpful in advancing the project.

I would also like to thank Marc Reisler of the law firm of Holland & Knight, who helped me with legal matters. In addition, I would like to single out Seth Perlman, General Counsel to Nonprofits at Perlman & Perlman, who serves as general counsel to a diverse nonprofit clientele.

Joe Sabrin
May 2015

Introduction by Abrashe Szabrinski

During WWII, our Jewish partisan fighters in the forests of eastern Europe fought shoulder to shoulder alongside the Soviet army from the east. We fought for the liberation of destroyed Vilna, Lithuania. On the day of liberation, approximately 15,000 Nazis were in captivity. About 1,500 Nazis were killed and wounded. The wounded were lying in the streets of Vilna like corpses. Vilna was ruined. The streets were empty. There were no more Jews in any of the houses. It was a dark and gloomy city. More than 60,000 Jews had been killed, including 10,000 who had been transported to the city from other communities.

Who were the fighters granted the right to take revenge for all the innocent Jewish blood? Who were those that fought for Jewish honor? They were the men and women of the Vilna ghetto. They were fifteen- and sixteen-year-olds who foresaw death for those who remained in the ghetto. They realized that the world had been torn away from them, and that they were torn away from the world. They came to the conclusion that their future lay in their own hands, and that if they must die, they would die with weapons in their hands.

They knew likewise that they had to organize into an underground movement. Even though it was difficult, they persisted, scraping together whatever weapons they could. Small groups were sent to the forest where a nascent partisan movement was born. People who had never heard a shot fired were taught the use of arms. They received military training and learned their lessons well. They became excellent fighters.

Then in the forest the Jews were given the opportunity to take revenge against the merciless murderers. If Warsaw is the symbol of Jewish destruction and Jewish heroism, Vilna is the symbol of Jewish revenge taken against the murderers.

The Jews in Vilna were ready to fight to their last breath, like their fellow Jews in Warsaw. On the last day of the ghetto's existence, the fighters were poised for war. They were ready to carry out the orders of their leaders. But rather than take on the Germans inside the ghetto and face immediate annihilation, orders were given to escape by means of the city's canals and reach the forests. There they could fight on.

Inside the ghetto, thousands of people, the old and infirm, were brought to Ponary, where they were executed and thrown into a pit. Healthy men and women were sent to the concentration camps of Estonia and then to Shtuthof. A few thousand were selected to work in Keilis or HKP (Heereskraftpark), camps inside Vilna's city limits. Along with the Estonia and Shtuthof concentration camps, these two Vilna camps were destroyed just before the city's liberation. Very few people lived through this terrible period.

The partisans of the forest knew about all the terrible travails of the remaining Vilna Jews and they were taking revenge by fighting a heroic battle. It required great effort to live in the forest. Hundreds of people needed food and clothing. We obtained these necessities from the surrounding villages, even though many of them actually received ammunition from the Germans in order to fight the partisans. These villages were in turn harshly punished or liquidated by the partisans. This task was assigned to men and women who once resided in the ghetto. Now, they took up arms and were fighting a life-and-death battle against their oppressors. This fight was not only directed against the Germans but also against the murderous White Poles, Ukrainians, and Lithuanians. They were aware that the Jewish bandits, as they called us, were a danger to the Germans.

The partisans were like a knife in the Germans' back. We blew up their trains. And because of this the Germans discontinued nightly train travel from Vilna to the cities of Kovno (Kaunus), Lida, and Maladzyechna. By day, too, they received their just rewards. The partisans cut dozens of telephone and telegraph wires. We closed the main highways. We burned their bridges.

But our encounters also cost a great many young Jewish lives. There is a long list of young people lost in action. Once a courageous young man named Joseph Glazman came to us in the forest with ten associates. They traveled 100 kilometers to reach a certain place. They were surrounded by a few hundred White Poles and killed. A partisan from Vilna, Rashl Markovitsh, a bright and heroic person, went out with a group of partisans in search of food from the surrounding villages. On the way back they were attacked by a large band of

Germans and Lithuanians. Rashl received a fiery bullet in her head and died a youthful death. Monyek Rodzyevitsh, a former student and intellectual, was a spy for us. He was part of our reconnaissance unit and because of this the Russians referred to him as a *"razvedchik"* [see note on *razvedka* in "Reconnaissance," chapter 8]. He was wounded and captured by Lithuanians. They tied him up by his feet to a sleigh. It was winter. He died while being pulled at a fast gallop by a group of horses. Imke Loybatski and four comrades were sent to cut telegraph lines. The Germans mined the poles that held up the wires. The partisans began to cut down the poles and were torn to shreds. Motl Gopstein, a good partisan, went out with a group of comrades to blow up a train. They carried out their mission, but were surrounded by Lithuanians. A battle began. Motl was shot in the stomach and yelled to his comrades to flee and that he would cover their escape. They did escape and then he shot himself in the head so as not to be captured alive by the bandits. He fulfilled his duty. In this manner the Jews of the Vilna ghetto fought the enemy. Vilna was not ashamed and Vilna did not shame the Jewish nation.

The fighters who were saved and those who perished for a holy cause are inscribed in the book of heroes of that dark period of Jewish destruction, a devastation that has no equal in any other era. These heroes are worthy of being called modern-day Maccabees. They fought for the honor of the Jewish nation. They doled out revenge against the murderous Germans.

I do not want to write my autobiography. I just want to share with everyone the hellish experiences that overtook me from September 1, 1939, to July 14, 1944. I am writing to honor and memorialize my heroic father Mayer Szabrinski; my clever and beautiful mother, Hana Leah Glick Szabrinski; my two sisters Fula and Henyele; and my three brothers Shloyme, Laybl, and Binyamin. Laybl and Binyamin perished while serving in the Red Army. I feel this task should be undertaken, completed, and assembled in a book. I hope my memory and spirit will serve me well to fulfill this holy obligation.

Abrashe Szabrinski, 1960

Chapter 1

"The battlefront disappeared, and with it the illusion that there had ever been a battlefront. For this was no war of occupation, but a war of quick penetration and obliteration – Blitzkrieg, Lightning War."

Time magazine, September 25, 1939[1]

"My wife, my children, and my wife's family died. Only I, Yudke, am alive, 'a log snatched from the fire,' a murmuring ember. My hands tremble and I am not in any condition to write of those terrible days."

Yehuda Vilechik[2]
Survivor of Kartuz-Bereza

Invasion

On September 1, 1939, Hitler's murderous army attacked Poland. With this act, the most ruthless murderer the world ever experienced set off WWII. The Jews paid heavily as a result of this war. The Jews paid with six million innocent sacrifices.

The Polish government mobilized all the men who were serving in the army. At that point, I had already served almost two years in an armed **folk regiment** in the city of Torun. I was also attached to a non-commissioned officers' school. I was an instructor for the new recruits. At the beginning of the war, I was mustered into a new people's artillery regiment. We were sent to Biala Podlaska, a town located not far from Brest Litovsk. When this unit, the Ninth Folk Regiment, arrived in the city, we received our assignments. Any astute individual could see that in a few weeks Poland would be no more.

NAZI-SOVIET INVASION

The Nazi invasion of Poland began on September 1, 1939. Then on September 17, the Soviets invaded from the east. Only weeks before, in late August of that year, Germany and Russia had signed the Ribbentrop-Molotov Pact, or non-aggression agreement, which contained secret clauses allowing for the division of eastern Europe into two spheres of influence. This marked the beginning of the Second World War, and the beginning of the Holocaust.[3]

FOLK REGIMENT

In his testimony for Yad Vashem, Abrashe mentioned that he had served in the Eighth People's Heavy Artillery. He further states that: "I was the only Jew in the unit of NCOs.... On the holidays I brought the other Jewish servicemen…a few hundred to the synagogue of Torun." (See appendix.)

The true Christian Poles, those who were interested in combat, wondered whether Hitler and Marshal Rydz-Smigli, the Commander-in-Chief of the Polish Armed Forces, shouldn't "slug it out." The Jews listened but did not respond. We took great pleasure from their words. Poland was an anti-Semitic country. In many of its cities, Jews were already living in ghettos. The Jews of Poland were well aware of the harsh conditions under which they were living.

On September 2, 1939, our folk regiment was ready for action. In the evening we boarded a train to bring us closer to the front. The Germans were advancing at a fast pace. Their tanks and artillery were moving at a speed of 30 kilometers per hour. Their artillery units were driving at the speed of 6 kilometers per hour. The Poles did not have tanks to equal those of the enemy. It was understood that we were up against the devil.

At lunchtime, I walked around the barracks of the Ninth Folk Regiment. I noticed that some of the mobilized soldiers were standing in a line. I approached them and asked: "Why are so many soldiers standing here?" They replied that many of the soldiers were very sick. I lined up with them as if I was also sick. What was the sickness that we imagined? We were all perfectly healthy and strong as steel. The popular sickness was venereal disease. When it was my turn to enter, I saw the doctor from a distance and recognized him. He was a Jew with the rank of lieutenant. My heart stopped pounding and I began to relax.

The doctor asked me what my malady was. I responded, "I am sick with a venereal disease." He examined me as if I really was ill. He told me that he would send me to a hospital in **Brisk**. This is what I wanted to hear. He gave me a document that I had to take to my superior officers stating that I should immediately be sent to a hospital. They became enraged but couldn't change the orders. About twenty or thirty soldiers were sent to Brisk, which is located 50 kilometers from Biala Podlaska.

My sister Fula lived in Brisk with her husband Chaim Kravits and their daughter. I went to visit them. My sister told me that she would lend me one of Chaim's suits. "You should change your clothes and wear a suit in my house."

BREST LITOVSK, OR BRISK as the Jews referred to it, is located 190 kilometers east of Warsaw at the intersection of the Bug and Mukhavets Rivers. In 1939, it was part of Poland. Now known as Brest, the city is in Belarus. By getting sent to Brisk, Abrashe found himself east of the Bug River [see note on the Bug River in "Invasion," chapter 1], which, after the invasion, would serve as the borderline between Soviet and Nazi occupied territory, putting him beyond Nazi reach for the time being.[4]

I told her that in a few days the Germans would be here, and that I would not remain because of the war. Also, I did not want to be labeled a deserter. I returned to the hospital, which was filled with soldiers. I was examined. A day later, a group of soldiers, myself included, was ordered to return to Biala Podlaska where our unit was stationed. When I returned, the unit was not there. They had been assigned to a place closer to the front. But we were not able to reach the front. The news on the radio was awful. An officer with the rank of lieutenant was with us. He was ordered to transport the soldiers. We were given guns. We were ordered to travel in the direction of **Kovel and Rivne**. From there we were supposed to go to **Romania** and from there, as soldiers of the Polish army, we would be sent to England.

KOVEL AND RIVNE are now located in Ukraine. Kovel is about 112 kilometers and Rivne about 241 kilometers southeast of Brisk.[5]

We arrived in Kovel, but couldn't go any further. The Red Army was nearing Rivne. Kovel had one railroad line that went to Brisk. About ten transport cars were parked in the railway yard. They were filled with soldiers and civilians who had escaped from the great cities of Warsaw and Siedlce. I encountered a group of Jewish soldiers from small towns in eastern Poland. The ten of us organized ourselves as a unit. They all came from Eastern Poland. The soldiers were residents of the following shtetls: Razshiniy, Bercze, Pruzhany and Seltz.

Many members of Poland's armed forces fled to ROMANIA. Marshal Rydz-Smigli himself took this route, but rather than continuing on to England, he returned to Poland to fight and later die of a heart attack. Poland maintained a government in exile that helped coordinate the Polish Home Army, which Abrashe would encounter later on. He calls them the "White Poles," and finds them both anti-Semitic and murderous.[6] [See note on White Poles in "The Forest," chapter 7.]

We decided that we must escape from Kovel. It was important to leave very quickly. In order to get out of town, we had to cross a bridge. But Polish policemen on horseback were stationed on the bridge to make sure that no one would escape the city. Our plan was to travel to Rivne and from there we would trek to Romania. If the Russians would try to stop us, we would fight back. But the only way to avoid the bridge was to swim across the **Bug River**.

The Bug was not a wide river, but it was very deep. We decided that we would attempt to cross to the other side that evening. I was one of the organizers of the mission. In the evening, we left our guns in a synagogue. We reached the river by way of a side street. It was very dark. It wasn't very cold but it also wasn't very warm. We completed the swim without any difficulty. We journeyed almost two kilometers and then turned in the direction of the railroad

THE BUG RIVER is about 40 kilometers west of Kovel. It was also the line of demarcation between Nazi and Soviet forces.[7]

tracks. There we found transports with all sorts of people from the surrounding area, most of them civilians on their way to Brisk. They weren't allowed to get into the transports. The Nazis and Russians were negotiating with each other. In a few days these transports left Brisk. Our group of Jewish soldiers found ourselves on the highway. We stopped some Red Army trucks and asked them for a lift to **Kartuz-Bereza**. The soldiers were very friendly toward us, and were willing to take us there. We arrived in Kartuz-Bereza and felt right at home. This was how our military service in the Polish army ended. A few weeks later, before our very eyes, we witnessed the destruction of the anti-Semitic Polish empire.

KARTUZ-BEREZA was founded in the seventeenth century and named for its numerous birch trees (bereza), and the nearby Carthusian Monastery. Its location along the Warsaw-Moscow road facilitated its early trade in horses and timber.

In July 1942, the Germans set up ghettos for the Jews: Ghetto A for productive Jews and Ghetto B for the rest. Both were destroyed in two *Aktions*. The first one took place on July 14–15, 1942. Under the pretense of taking the Jews to a nearby city for work, the Nazis sent the inhabitants of Ghetto B to Brona Gura, where pits had been prepared, and shot them to death. The second *Aktion*, which effectively annihilated the Jewish population of Kartuz-Bereza, began on October 15, 1942. The SS surrounded the ghetto and many of the inhabitants, certain that this signaled the end, burned their belongings. The fire spread to several buildings, and the ghetto continued burning throughout the night. Many others took up arms and were killed. The members of the Judenrat and their families committed suicide by hanging themselves. The following day the Nazis took those who remained alive and shot them on a nearby hill.[8]

Seltz

Everyone was overjoyed when I arrived in my hometown, **Seltz**, situated ten kilometers from Kartuz-Bereza. My parents, three brothers, and a sister were the first ones to greet me. My other sister Fula and her husband found out that I had returned to Seltz a day later. They all joked about my undistinguished combat performance. I lost Poland to the enemy, they said. But in reality Poland had already been divided between Hitler's Germany and Russia. A large number of Russians were already stationed in the city. They behaved in a proper manner. The headquarters for all of their administrative departments was located in the former Polish *Volksschule*, which had once upon a time served as the police station.

SELTZ was a small shtetl not far from Brisk and about 96 kilometers southwest of Baranovich. It is now part of Belarus. In his book, *A Voyage of Mission from Moscow to Poland* (1678), the diplomat Bernard Tanner described Seltz as "a city built of wood and full of Jews." The Germans captured the town on June 23, 1941, the second day of their invasion of Russia. The Jews of Seltz were brought to Kartuz-Bereza on May 25, 1942.[9]

My two brothers and I went to **Baranovich**. One brother was a baker, the other one was a tailor, and I was a locksmith. When we got there, we were assigned an apartment and giv-

BARANOVICH is located some 193 kilometers northeast of Brisk. "Up until the first slaughter [by the Nazis] there were about 12,000 Jews in Baranovich." Abrashe discusses Baranovich in detail below.[10]

en work. We sent back food that was not available in our hometown. Life in Baranovich also became very difficult. There was an influx of young Jews from the other [western] side of the Bug River, where the Germans were in control. These refugees were called Byezshintes [see note on Byezshintes in "Two Camps," chapter 4]; a great many of them would go back and forth across the river, since they could not decide where to remain. Should they live under Russian or German rule? At this point in time, the Germans had not revealed their murderous faces, and the Jews did not want to believe in Hitler's *Mein Kampf*. The Soviets required the Jews to carry Soviet passports and become Soviet citizens. Some Jews refused to do so and the Soviets restricted their movements, forbidding them to cross from one side of the river to the other. Many thousands of Jews were sent deep into Russia. Ironically, however, it was their good fortune to be held captive in the USSR. They were able to live through the ordeals and survive the destruction of European Jewry. Even though they endured hardships, it was better than a death sentence under the Nazis.

In the beginning of the sixth month, in the year 1940, my two brothers Laybl and Binyamin were drafted into the Red Army. Binyamin was twenty-two years old and Laybl was twenty. Binyamin served in a Kaleynan Unit, which in English would be called the Marines. He was stationed at the front. Laybl was sent to the city of Chelyabinsk where he was a radio technician. I was mobilized into the 405th Artillery Regiment, which was stationed in **Stolftsi**, located about 50 kilometers east of Baranovich. Hundreds of former Polish soldiers were mobilized along with me. The Red Army needed to retrain them. I was an artillery instructor and was able to train the unit since I was fluent in Polish. I am sure that the Soviet artillery units were more experienced than the Polish ones. All the instructions were short and the calculations exact. We, the former reservists, were called up for a half a year after which we were sent home. The reservist's pay was contingent upon the assignment he was given.

Upon ending my tour of duty, I worked as a locksmith at the sawmill that had previously belonged to Yosel Yevitshn in Baranovich. The Soviets had

STOLFTSI is probably the town of Stoibtz, which survivor Motl Machtai claimed had more names than any other shtetl in the area. It was known variously as "Stoibtz, Shtoibtz, Stulbtz, Stulptzi, etc." Of a total population of about 8,000, the Jews numbered 3,000. It was founded in the fifteenth or sixteenth century on the banks of the Niemen River. Almost all of the town's Jews were exterminated by the Nazis. And according to Getzel Reiser several survivors were sent to Baranovich.[11]

nationalized it. I often received letters from my two brothers. They were happy serving in the Soviet army. The Jews did not feel that they were second-class citizens and there were plenty of Jewish officers. My brothers were thinking of attending officers' school or an officers' academy. They were ambitious and brave. The months passed by without any incidents. All this changed due to the calamity that came upon us.

Hitler's murderous army attacked Russia. I am sure that the Soviets knew that war was inevitable. They built various kinds of side roads. They employed tens of thousands of workers, most of them prisoners who had been sentenced for political crimes. Their political views did not coincide with those of the Communist Party. They were simply categorized as counter-revolutionaries and made to work or worse.

In the evening of the day that the war broke out, I received a mobilization card. I was ordered to immediately report to the draft board. When I arrived at 8:00 AM, there were already hundreds of reservists present. The majority of them were former Polish soldiers. I reported to the officer who gave me the list of 200 names. They were all artillery specialists. I was to join up with the 405th Regiment. They had been in Stolftsi, but were now in Lisnic, which is 25 kilometers west of Baranovich. I pleaded with the officer telling him that he should give me a few vehicles so that we could reach our assigned regiment quickly. He replied that no vehicles were available and we had to go on foot. We had no choice. We finally arrived at the place where our regiment was stationed. I had no idea how long the trek would be. We often had to flee into the forest to avoid detection by German airplanes.

When we arrived at our destination, two Russian officers greeted us. They ordered me to lead our unit toward **Minsk** so we could join up with the regiment. I understood that such an action was a losing proposition. We would not be able to display the discipline of the reservists. Among the roster of soldiers that I had under me, there were a fair number of Jews. I was responsible for them.

MINSK The city is located some 145 kilometers northeast of Baranovich as the crow flies. Abrashe's assessment that he could not reach Minsk was probably correct.[12]

We started walking in the direction of Baranovich. There were vehicles passing us by. They were carrying wounded soldiers and moving at a very fast pace. The German planes were bombing the roads. We were amazed that we did not see any Russian planes in the air. After walking with my unit for a while, I decided to separate myself from them. They could go wherever they desired. I knew we couldn't reach Minsk and my conclusion was correct. When small groups of us arrived in Baranovich, we found the city center in flames. The Soviet army was nowhere to be seen. A day later the German army entered the city.

When I observed German military power, I concluded that the Soviet army couldn't match them in battle. My body shuddered when I saw the mechanized unity of the German forces: the tanks, the artillery, the mechanized squadrons, and their airplanes.

We should be amazed at the bravery of the Russian people. The Germans wanted to destroy them with their great might, but they weren't successful, although the Russian people paid a very dear price. The Russians are to be admired for their heroism and resiliency. They were fighting the mighty Germans for years and in the end they were victorious. I witnessed these events, and it is proper that I should record these moments for all to know. I witnessed Hitler's army marching with their heads up high and I also witnessed their downfall. The Russian people had to support one another to make up for individual, physical and mental illnesses.

Years later, in the city of Vilna, the partisans and the Red Army would fight together. German bodies were scattered around the city. Most of them were members of the SS, Hitler's elite fighting machine. Thousands of soldiers were captured and imprisoned. We found them hiding in cellars and pulled them out. The partisans disarmed them completely. The Germans had Jewish belongings and artifacts with them. As a commander, I allowed my units to gather the spoils of war. Now let us return to earlier events.

My Father and the Fate of Seltz

My father, Mayer, the son of Binyamin Szabrinski, was born in 1890 in Seltz, a small town in the province of Grodno. He worked as a saddle maker, but he did not bring home a lot of money. He was a simple man, with a wife and six children, four boys and two girls. Three sons, myself included, were soldiers in the Red Army in 1941.

Aside from one married sister who lived in Brisk, my entire family was living in Seltz when the Nazis occupied the area. Our shtetl was too small for the Nazis to section off a Jewish ghetto, therefore, the Jews were transported to Kartuz-Bereza, ten kilometers away. When I returned to my hometown in 1946, I was told the facts about my father's life during the German occupation. The local anti-Semites persecuted him. They wanted to know the whereabouts of his sons. There were Poles who worked with the Germans and eventually became policemen in the shtetl. Three of these individuals, Stanislav Burdzvik, Myetshislov Vrublyevski, and Stakh Zdanavitsh, were executed by the partisans.

In 1942, the forests, including the great Rozshinoyer (Ružany) Forest, located not far from Seltz and Kartuz-Bereza, were beginning to be infiltrated by small groups of **Russian partisans**. They had connections with the outside, but to carry out their operations they needed information about German movements. My father would receive information from a Pole. His name was Stanislav Yakubtshik, and he was a true socialist and a good friend to the Jews. Yakubtshik worked as a secretary in the office of the German military commandant in Kartuz-Bereza. A Jewish girl, Dora Kaplan, worked with him in the office.

Dealing with RUSSIAN PARTISANS in the forests of Belarus was life threatening, particularly for a Jew. Numerous firsthand accounts make it plain that these partisans were not well-disposed toward Jews and killed them with regularity. It was unlikely for any Jew who escaped the Nazis and their ghettos to survive among the forest partisans on their own, especially without weapons.[13]

She had been born in Seltz in 1914. She was the only child of Meir and Sarah Kaplan. Her father was a butcher by trade. The Kaplan family was well respected in our town. Dora received instruction in Jewish studies from a private tutor and was also a student in the Polish *Volksschule* in Seltz. After she concluded her studies in the *Volksschule*, her parents sent her to the gymnasium in Brisk. Dora was a pretty, intelligent, and knowledgeable young lady. She was even respected by the Polish intelligentsia, who were not friendly to the Jews. The Soviets had assigned Dora to the Post and Telephone Bureau. She kept this position until the Soviets and the Germans began their war. When the Germans occupied Seltz, she shared the destiny of all the other Jews.

As fate would have it, when the Jews of Seltz were transported to Kartuz-Bereza and forced into the ghetto, Stanislav Yakubtshik, who Dora knew very well, was assigned the position of secretary of Polish matters in the German commandant's office in Kartuz-Bereza. As a gentile, and because of his position, he had the right to have a servant for his family. This was how Dora came to work for him as his servant.

In 1942, the forests were beginning to be infiltrated by small groups of partisans. Rozshinoyer Forest was close to Seltz and Kartuz-Bereza, and Stanislav Yakubtshik, because of his position in the commandant's office, knew all the German orders and movements. He wrote the information on thin cigarette papers, which he would give to Dora. She would conceal the papers in her thick black hair and then deliver them to my father. My father would then transfer them to farmers who had contact with the partisans.

On June 19, 1942, when Dora was leaving her place of work to go back to the ghetto, the Gestapo arrested her. They found the paper with the information and began to torture her bitterly. She divulged the names of my father and Yakubtshik. They experienced extreme torture. They were all shot and buried in one grave in the monastery of Kartuz-Bereza.

This was how my father, Dora Kaplan, and Stanislav Yakubtshik met their ends. They are remembered with great respect. I wrote the complete story and gave it to Yad Vashem. All of this information was recorded in the *Leksikon Hagevurah*, volume 2, published by Yad Vashem in Israel. When I was in Seltz in 1964, I retold the story to fine gentiles who I knew, Alga Skrobat and Stefan Panasevitsh.

Chapter 2

*"From the train they boarded trucks that had benches. I do not
know the number of people a truck could accommodate. They
boarded the trucks and were driven away. The Czech Jews were
gassed to death in these trucks. In ten minutes they all died."*

Abrashe Szabrinski

The Occupation of Baranovich

When the Germans entered **Baranovich**, they grabbed people for various work details. Some were assigned to clean army machinery to ensure that it would perform with precision.

A few days later, the SS arrived in the city. We immediately experienced their murderous orders, among them the decree that Jews were not permitted to receive pay for their work. We were not allowed to walk on the sidewalks, only in the middle of the streets. After that the Gestapo issued more decrees against the Jews. Then the murderous Wagner arrived in Baranovich. He had been the first commandant of the Dachau concentration camp, situated near Landsberg, Germany. We later discovered that **Schlegel**, the chief of the Gestapo, had also come to the city.

The order came to construct a Jewish ghetto. All the Jews of Baranovich were to be concentrated in one place. There were 12,000 Jews in the town, including the "Byezshintes" [see note on Byezshintes in "Two Camps," chapter 4], who had escaped from other cities and sought safety in Baranovich. **Izakson** was

The Nazis occupied **BARANOVICH** on June 27, 1941. Shmuel Yankelewicz, a Baranovich survivor, notes that the Nazis immediately seized 400 victims upon entering the city. The Jewish community then raised money for the return of the 400. The Nazis took the money but did not return the people. Such was the behavior of Germans all over eastern Europe. They were not content with merely murdering their victims; they also sought to steal everything of value from them in the process.[1]

SCHLEGEL was the Gestapo commander who organized the first slaughter (also known as the Purim Slaughter [see note below on 6,000 ghetto Jews]). Later he had the Jews assemble before the Judenrat and explained that the slaughter was over and normal life would begin.[2]

In the extant accounts **IZAKSON** is remembered as an honest and decent man who executed his loathsome task as "Jewish Elder" with humanity, always seeking to aid the Jews rather than collaborate with the Nazis.

Eliezer Lidowsky recalls: "When I first returned to Baranovich…Izakson came to me and said, 'the Gestapo is demanding two locksmiths, and if not, there will be victims.' He beseeched me, and one other person not to refuse him, and in order to raise our spirits, he came along with us, and took the first of the beatings."[3]

JEWISH POLICE

Zuckerman is not mentioned in the extant record with respect to this position. Chaim Weltman was made the "commandant of the Jewish police in the ghetto." Pinchas Mordkowsky recalls that Weltman was a craftsman and activist, but that he was killed along with all of his police. He was ordered by the Germans to provide twenty-five of his police for a work detail. Chaim reasoned that his men would be killed if he allowed them to be separated. He therefore insisted that all his men be sent together as one unit instead. He believed the Germans would refuse to take the whole body of police and would therefore take none; or, that if the Germans did take his whole force they would surely not kill them all. However, the Germans took him along with all his men and killed them at the Green Bridge. Mordkowsky does not give a date for this action.[4]

chosen to head the ghetto committee. He was a brilliant person and a lawyer by profession. Zuckerman, a Jew, was appointed as the head of the **Jewish police**.

We began our ghetto existence. In the beginning, we went to our jobs without escorts. Jews worked everywhere and at different types of jobs. I was working in Yosel Yevitshn's lumber factory. There were about eighty Jewish workers. The manager of the factory was a Pole by the name of Kallaynski and the owner was V. Fred Wegener. A Pole named Balkhan managed certain buildings and houses. Both were soldiers. They were respectful toward the Jews.

I was employed as a locksmith, but I wanted to work at other types of jobs away from the lumber factory. I wanted to transport beams from the old railroad station so I solicited one of the administrators of the Kallaynski Lumber Factory and was assigned a job I desired. Two other Jews worked along with me at transporting the beams, Israel Berkowitz and Berel Rabinovitch. I changed my work station for three reasons. The first was that I wanted to hear the latest news from the gentiles; the second was that outside the ghetto I could buy food or barter clothing; and finally, I had more freedom of movement.

We were required to wear a yellow band on our clothing, but at work we were able to use all the facilities without wearing it. We lived our lives in this manner until a new decree was issued, which stipulated that Jews were not permitted to leave work without an escort. We had a premonition that something was going to take place in the ghetto, but we did not know what it was. Izakson, the head of the ghetto board, assured us that he knew of nothing imminent. While we were transporting beams, we witnessed a terrible event.

A group of Jews from Czechoslovakia arrived at the old Baranovich train station. That week Czechs were watching the transports but they were wearing SS uniforms. We spoke with them. They told us that 3,000 Jews were arriving in Baranovich. They were being transported from Czechoslovakia. The group included men and women who had a contract for one year's work in the east. After the year was up they would return home.

They were rich Jews. Most of them were professionals: doctors, lawyers, and important businessmen. The men and women were dressed nicely. They had with them a large amount of luggage, valises, and many types of packages. We all believed what they told us. The Czechs were honorable people. They themselves believed the story they were telling us. The train cars had special types of seats for these passengers. There was food and drink. In Baranovich, they were to disembark and be led to hotels with restaurants. The passengers would then freshen up and eat. Once refreshed, they would continue on their journey.

I will now state what really happened to these poor souls. They arrived on nice transports. From the train, they boarded trucks that had benches. I do not know the number of people a truck could accommodate. They boarded the trucks and were driven away. The Czech Jews were gassed to death in these trucks (**mobile death vans**). In ten minutes they all died. They prepared holes in the ground three kilometers from the train station. The Nazis threw the naked bodies in the holes. The real SS performed these deeds. They did not trust anybody else to carry out their orders. They suspected that money and gold objects were sewn into the Jewish clothing. Their hunch was correct. Hidden in the clothing of these very wealthy individuals, they did indeed find rich treasures. The sixty Czech escorts were also taken to the holes and shot dead. The SS did not want any witnesses to their treachery. In a span of five hours all were dead. The Germans performed all the tasks with total efficiency.

FIRSTHAND ACCOUNT:

DR. ZELIK LEVINBOOK RECALLED:

"On that day, a transport departed from the rear of the platform of the Baranovich station containing 3,000 Czech Jews.... After stopping the train, it was related that now is the time for the midday meal. They accept this as self-explanatory.... Freight trucks then come by and everyone gets in, as well as the Czech train escorts – and the trucks ride off. Among these trucks are also a large number of vehicles with hermetically sealed doors. The Baranovich Gestapo...takes all this – the Jewish Czech intelligentsia: doctors, dentists, engineers, architects, teachers, jurists, and rabbis, all with their families. They are taken to the 'midday meal' in the 'Gai' woods behind New Baranovich to the northeast of Zhlobin Lake. Pits have already been dug out there in advance. The newly arrived Jews are ordered to disrobe, gather all their clothing in one spot – after that, they are all shot, standing on the lip of the pit. The hermetically sealed trucks, called 'Dushegubkehs' (from the Russian for soul-exterminators) bring victims that are finished already, which do not require being shot: they were poisoned by gas, and smoke, which exhausts from the truck motor, after burning the benzine fuel. The exhaust fumes, normally discharged into the air, are channeled into these trucks through a special pipe and in this fashion the people inside are asphyxiated by fumes.... In this instance as well, the murderers do not begrudge the dead their clothing. Also, the Christian Czech conductors are shot."[7]

MOBILE DEATH VANS were one of the more invidious inventions of the German death machine and one of the early means used to implement the "final solution." They were large vans whose cargo bays were lined with benches. The exhaust from the engine was piped into the cargo area and the occupants were gassed to death. Several accounts claim many of these vans were disguised as Red Cross vehicles. [5]

In his article in the *Baranovich Memorial Book*, Shmuel Yankelewicz mentions this or a similar atrocity. According to his account, however, the Czech Jews were taken to the woods and shot. He states that, "On one occasion, a transport carrying 3,000 Czech Jews was unloaded from the train and shot in the nearest woods...."[6]

The clothing and packages were brought to large warehouses belonging to the SS. Jewish workers employed there sorted the items with German exactness. Most of them were women from the Vilna ghetto. I knew a great many of them. Quite a few put their lives in danger by smuggling diamonds out of the warehouses and bringing them to the ghetto. The booty was then transferred to the underground fighting organizations and used to buy ammunition from certain Poles. The precious cargoes were hidden in bottles of spices and in large challahs, which the women baked themselves. This episode occurred in April 1942. I am quite sure of the date.

In Vilna, the JUDENRAT, or Jewish ghetto councils established by the Nazis, would suffer from the same denial demonstrated in Baranovich. Again and again the Judenrats of the various ghettos were offered proof of what the Germans were truly up to, but they ignored what they were told and shown. In most cases the truth was too terrible to come to terms with. The German actions were so far outside the pale of historical precedence that it was difficult to comprehend that they were truly aiming to exterminate all of European Jewry. "The Germans would not kill us all," is a sentiment that led many to their graves. [8]

In his memoir about Vilna, Joseph Foxman wrote, "People preferred to believe the 'good' things rather than the unthinkable news that the deported Jews were no longer alive."[9]

After this catastrophe, the **Judenrat** was informed about what happened to the Czech Jews. We told them about it, since we had been in the vicinity of this massacre. Good Christians who were shocked by this event, also reported to the Judenrat about what had transpired at the railroad station. The Jews heard many rumors about the episode, but they did not want to believe it. They felt that there was no foundation to these rumors. They did not want to believe that the Germans were murdering Jews. Faith in the Germans misled the Jewish community and eventually led them into a dangerous situation.

Less than two months later, Schlegel, the head of the Gestapo, visited the Judenrat's office. He ordered **Izakson** to gather together 3,000 Jews. Izakson's response was as follows: "I have given you gold, silver and dairy products." These were taxes the Germans placed on the Jewish community. "I will not deliver any Jews to you."

Dr. Zelik Levinbook recalls that when IZAKSON was asked to hand over Jews to the Nazis he said, "I have given you everything, everything you have asked of me, but Jews – I will not give you, because I am not the master of human lives." The Germans, on the other hand, believed they were the masters of human life and that in the name of "race" they had the right to "engineer" the human population by eliminating those who their ideology deemed *untermensch*, i.e., sub-human.[10]

Schlegel left the office. In the morning, SS soldiers, White Russians, and Ukrainian policemen surrounded the ghetto. The White Russians and Ukrainians worked devotedly for the Germans. On this day, the Germans and their allies would murder **6,000 ghetto Jews.**

While the slaughter was going on, many Jews were at their places of work. The workers of Yosel Yevitshn's lumber factory were also at their jobs when the ghetto was surrounded. After we learned what had happened, we convened a meeting to decide how to react. With the consent of the entire factory, we decided not to return to the ghetto. Our lumber factory was an important source of production for the Germans.

Two German officers administered the factory. Both of them had been wounded at the front. One had the rank of captain and the other was a lieutenant. At the meeting, two Jewish workers were assigned to inform the two Germans about what had happened. One delegate was Freylim Itskovitch, whose father was a bookkeeper at the factory. I was the second delegate.

We went to the office, a house not far from the lumber factory, and found one of them there. When he saw us, his face turned white as snow. He understood why we were there. We informed him that we knew what was taking place in the ghetto. He told us what he knew. He mentioned that he had attended a meeting with the District Commander Wagner, who stated that those employed in skilled jobs would remain unharmed. We thanked him and relayed our conversation to our fellow workers. Together we decided to remain at the factory for another day and not return to the ghetto.

We heard the screaming.

Some Incidents That Occurred during the *Aktion*

A German sergeant serving in the Luftwaffe fell in love with a Jewish girl from the ghetto. When things in the ghetto were normal, he would come every evening on his motorcycle to visit her. When he found out that an **Aktion** was going to take place in the

---

6,000 GHETTO JEWS: THE PURIM SLAUGHTER

Tuesday, March 3, 1942, began as any other day in the ghetto, but by early afternoon something was amiss. Some Jews had already begun to be held back at the main gate on their way to work. Suddenly a truck full of armed Germans pulled inside the ghetto. Outside the walls Belarussians and Lithuanians surrounded the ghetto in force. From all accounts the Germans divided the ghetto into two groups: those with a "life pass" and those without. This "life pass" was distributed by forcing all Jews to walk through a narrow passage where the Nazi Max Krampe stood handing out passes based on his spot assessment of "usefulness." During the night, the head of the Judenrat, Izakson, intervened on behalf of the ghetto so that more passes were distributed. At 6:00 AM the next morning the Germans and their accomplices began to remove those who did not have passes. The last to be taken was Evsei Izakson, the Ghetto Elder, and his secretary Zhenya Mann. When the Germans fell short of their quota, they began taking those with "life passes."[11]

Aktion is a German word, which in the context of the Holocaust typically means the mass removal of Jews from a ghetto, town, or city for any purpose whatsoever, including removal for work or to be murdered.[12]

ghetto, he went there to save her life. When he got there he was told that she had been taken away on a truck with other Jews. The Germans were going to kill those who had been caught. He found out where she had been taken and went to find her. She was at the **Green Bridge**. He went to see Schlegel, the head of the Gestapo, and pleaded with him to return his girlfriend. The murderous Schlegel responded as follows: "From here, no one returns! Do you want to be killed with her?" They killed the German along with his Jewish girlfriend. This is a true story. A White Russian policeman recounted it to me after the *Aktion*.

THE GREEN BRIDGE stood at a crossing of the Warsaw/Moscow and Vilna/Lemberg railroad lines. The Warsaw line passed over the Vilna tracks. The Germans took the victims of the Purim Slaughter to a spot not far from the bridge and shot them while they were standing on the edge of the pits that had been prepared beforehand.[13]

*   *   *

Another incident that took place during the *Aktion* involved **Manye**, a pianist, as well as a very pretty woman. She had a son who was seven years old. She was married to an older man who sold lumber and was very rich. When the Soviets came to Baranovich, he was introduced to them as one of the wealthy citizens of the city. She lived in a large house and rented out rooms to two military families. Mayor Gratshov, the Commissar of the entire Commissariat of Baranovich, was the head of one these families. He held a high position with many duties. He had a wife by the name of Shuraa and a daughter, Leyalye. They came from the city of Novosibirsk. Thanks to Manye, I became very friendly with them. I was like a member of their family.

MANYE

Dr. Zelik Levinbook wrote about the first mass slaughter in Baranovich, known as the Purim Slaughter, which took place at the beginning of March 1942. He stated, "When the family of Dr. Nakhumowsky was already on the truck, a senior officer of the SD took note of the doctor's sister-in-law, Manye, who was a laundress in the SD laundry. The officer designates that she should be taken off the truck. He wants to save her, but she sets a condition that he must take her entire family, together with her seven-year-old little boy, to which he does not agree. Then she shouts out, 'You filthy dogs! You, your wives, and children, your entire nation will pay with your blood for our innocent blood and that of our children that you have spilled.' Her words are cut short by a beating and the truck moves on, leaving the ghetto."[14]

The second family was made up of a captain, his wife, and children. Manye and her son required two rooms. Everyone shared the kitchen. Manye washed the Gestapo's clothes. During the *Aktion*, Manye and her son were transported to the ghetto. The Gestapo wanted to save her from death. They needed her to wash their clothing. They proposed that Manye be allowed to leave the truck that was loaded with people, but without her son. She spat in the face of one of the Gestapo officers and was, therefore, sent to her death. This was a true story witnessed by the people from the ghetto.

The Finality of the *Aktion*

The last one to be shot was the important lawyer and chairman of the Judenrat, **Izakson**. His sin was that he refused to voluntarily deliver Jews to be killed by the Germans. Zuckerman was the chief of the ghetto police. Schlegel ordered him to gather all the Jewish police. He wanted them to straighten out the dead bodies. After completing their task, they were all killed. A former motorcycle policeman from Baranovich was able to **hide** and remained alive.

The Green Bridge, where they shot 6,000 of Baranovich's Jews, was not far from the sawmill, less than two kilometers away. In the morning we returned to the ghetto. It had the appearance of a large cemetery. We knew that life must go on and indeed life did return in the ghetto. We were now living under the rule and might of the murderous Germans.

This was how the first *Aktion* ended in Baranovich. The murderous Germans of the murderous German nation carried it out.

IZAKSON'S DEATH

"A taxi pulls up to the Judenrat building. Krampe goes over to the 'Jewish Elder' (Izakson) and to his lady assistant, and accosts them with his riding crop, which in this instance signifies death. He orders them to be put into the taxi, and they are conveyed to the pits."[15]

Like the leaders of other ghettos, Dr. Izakson, who headed the Baranovich Judenrat, was in a unique position to be hated, but he did not feel that collaboration was part of his duties. As in other firsthand accounts, Abrashe Szabrinski has nothing but praise for this man who was in an impossible position. In a previous life, Mr. Yehoshua Izakson was the head of the Merchants' Union in Baranovich.[16]

Already by the time of the first slaughter, a large number of Jews managed to successfully **HIDE** in bunkers and a variety of other hiding places. This provided an impetus to the residents of the ghetto to complete the construction of bunkers. Dozens of systems, one more clever than the next, were employed in the building of 'living graves and caves' for oneself, under the surface of the earth."[17]

Chapter 3

"The ghetto – dead empty. On the ground, the bodies of the dead
lay strewn about. The single small horse in the ghetto – as scrawny
as a skeleton walked around among the dead bodies…"

Eliezer Lidowsky, survivor of the Baranovich extermination[1]

Liquidation

After the great *Aktion*, Wagner, the area commander, ordered the Jews to select **another
Judenrat**. This was needed to create stability
in the ghetto. A new president was elected, a
certain Yankelewicz. I do not know anything
about his background. The talk was that he was
from the business world. The ghetto, once
again, began to function.

The Jews returned to their jobs. **The work
representatives** picked up the columns of Jews
in the morning. In the evenings they were
brought back to the ghetto, which was guarded
by German as well as Jewish policemen. We
were not allowed to bring food into the ghetto,
but we were able to overcome the hardships.
The Jews knew that their labor was for the
devil. There was no future with these jobs. As
long as the Germans needed Jewish labor then
the ghetto was quiet. We knew we were on the
road to destruction.

Organized **underground groups** were established in the ghetto. I knew about two of them.

ANOTHER JUDENRAT

The Purim Slaughter marked the end for the Jews of
Baranovich. As Eliezer Lidowsky recalls, "It was a sign
that the prior period, and its methods of operation
[were] dead. Nevertheless, the new Judenrat learned
nothing from this." Up to this point, the inhabitants
of the Baranovich ghetto lived under the false notion
that somehow their town was different and they
would be spared.[2]

WORK REPRESENTATIVES

It was in the uniform of these "work representatives"
that Gestapo men were able to execute the Second
Slaughter. They did so by drawing away the daily
quota of men for work outside the ghetto, while
demanding the addition of three hundred men. This
effectively drained the ghetto of a large portion of
the men who could fight.[3]

UNDERGROUND GROUP

As with the underground organization in the Vilna
Ghetto, the Baranovich partisans organized themselves into cells. Individual members would know of
no one outside their own group unless they themselves were the group leader. Members were also
obliged to take an oath which declared, "I swear by
those of our own who have fallen, and those who
remain alive, that I will exact revenge from the fascist murderers, will serve loyally to accomplish the
objectives of the fighting organization, and carry out
its orders unquestioningly. If I should betray this oath,
let the hand that punishes render its judgment."[4]

These were very **secret organizations**, made up of cells with no more than five people. Not everyone knew his or her own leaders. The person who recommended me was a good friend of mine, Yehezkel the locksmith. I knew that our leader was Dr. Berkowitz. He was the brother of Israel Berkowitz, with whom I worked at the sawmill.

In four to six weeks, we possessed guns and grenades in the ghetto. There were many ways of smuggling in the ammunition. An amazing amount of ammunition was stored in Israel Berkowitz's house, which was owned by the police. I lived in a house that belonged to Yosel the carpenter. In the evenings, we would clean the guns and teach our comrades how to use them. The goal was to establish a resistance movement in the event the Germans would initiate another *Aktion*. I did not agree with this strategy. It made no sense to me. I thought it was important to establish ties with the partisans who were in the forest.

The two underground organizations in the ghetto had already decided that if another *Aktion* took place, they would burn down the entire ghetto and shoot any German soldier they could. The people who escaped would flee to wherever they could find a safe hiding place. We continually discussed these plans, about which there were many opinions.

I already knew that within the ghetto there were hundreds of guns and dozens of grenades. The Gestapo understood that young people would organize themselves into fighting units. There were informers in the ghetto. I could not determine the veracity of the information that I possessed since I was not personally informed about the matter.

Many months passed [see **timeline**] and the ghetto returned to normal, as before the first *Aktion*. I do not know how many months went by. The Jewish workers continued to be taken to work in the factory, all of us leaving together in the usual formation of columns. Then one day the Germans who led us to work were dressed in the uniforms of

---

SECRET ORGANIZATIONS

Eliezer Lidowsky organized the partisan group in Baranovich two weeks after the Purim Slaughter. Describing its establishment, he says, "The plan was built on personal contact with people who had an idealistic upbringing.... Four groups of five (twenty people) formed a division, and a commander was placed in charge of them. A staff commander headed five divisions (one hundred people). The activities were intensely conspiratorial."[5]

TIMELINE

In January 1943, Baranovich survivor Herman Kruk, a former lawyer from Warsaw, whose wife and child were killed during the second *Aktion*, wrote this TIMELINE: "Up until the 'cleansing,' there were about 12,000 Jews in Baranovich. The first 'cleansing' took place on March 4, 1942, and lasted that [entire] day. Four thousand Jews were killed. About 8,000 souls remain[ed] in the city.

"The second 'cleansing' took place a day after Yom Kippur, Tuesday, September 22, 1942. This 'cleansing' lasted for eight days. Of those eight thousand Jews that had remained alive up until that point, approximately an additional 5,000 were killed. Therefore, in Baranovich, only 3,000 Jews remained alive.

"The third 'cleansing' began on December 17, 1942, and lasted three days. The result of this is that to date, in January 1943, there are up to 200 [Jews] alive."[6]

the **Todt** organization. We were a few thousand workers, and we were brought to the office of the area commander, Wagner.

The Germans executed their well-thought-out **plans** with exactness. They outsmarted the Jews. They chose a thousand young Jews. Among them were about fifty somewhat older people. I was among them. I was standing next to Yudel Vishnya. I said to him: "I will run to the ghetto. This is another slaughter." Yudel was a family man. He had a wife and three children. He told me to be calm. "**They are only taking people to their jobs**," he said, and I listened to him.

We were brought together and then placed in different columns. White Russian police led us to the train station. They told us that we must walk near a prison. The Jews in the columns immediately organized themselves. One person would update another with the latest information. If they led us in the direction of the prison, we planned to throw ourselves on the guards who were surrounding us. Those that could escape would do so.

We went by the prison on the way to the train station. They prepared vehicles for us to board. A senior member of Todt told us that we were traveling to perform new work. The place we were headed for was not far from Old Vilayke. Once there, we would rebuild the railroad tracks leading toward the Soviet Union. The Soviet tracks were wide and the German tracks were narrow. This was all true. "We do not destroy people" [he said]. "We want people to work."

TODT was a German construction firm organized along military lines. Its founder and namesake, Fritz Todt, was an ardent Nazi supporter who was rewarded for his support with the contract to build the Autobahn, a project that allowed his relatively small company to become transformed into one of the largest in Germany by the middle of the 1930s. As the Nazis conquered their neighbors, Todt was used for the construction of various projects from the Atlantic Wall to V-2 rocket launching platforms, and the conversion of Russian gauge railroad tracks to German tracks. As the war progressed, Todt began using forced labor from the conquered territories.[7]

By dressing in the Todt uniforms, the Gestapo men deceived the Jews and were able to carry out the Second Slaughter with less resistance than they might have otherwise encountered.[8]

PLANS: THE SECOND SLAUGHTER

One survivor describes what happened after Abrashe and many other men were sent outside the ghetto gates that day: "The wild bloodthirsty animals, being Germans of all sorts, Russians, Poles, and others – ran around with their hunting dogs, all over the ghetto, looking for and sniffing out blood and victims.

"When the slaughter was halted, we went up to the attic. We then looked around on all sides and it was here that the terrifying image was laid out before us, a *bona fide* battlefield. The ghetto – dead empty. On the ground, the bodies of the dead lay strewn about. The single small horse in the ghetto – as scrawny as a skeleton – whose owner had been killed, walked around among the dead bodies, and searched for grass to eat (in the over-trampled crowding of the ghetto, grass did not grow). The houses had been pillaged, the window panes smashed, the open doors and windows banged back and forth in the autumn wind.

"Around the continuous barbed-wire containment of the ghetto, stood thousands of gentiles, including among them the elderly, women and children, with sacks in their hands, and, like barnyard fowl, were chomping at the bit to plunder."[9]

"THEY ARE ONLY TAKING PEOPLE TO THEIR JOBS."

Eliezer Lidowsky wrote: "…the 'Todt' personnel offered the explanation that they are here solely to fill out the contingent of an additional 300 Jews."[10]

We traveled a while and then, after an entire night, arrived at **Old Vilayke**. They had a large barracks that housed 700 men. I was among a group of 300 people. We walked ten kilometers further east of Old Vilayke. Here we had to build a barrack. The components were assembled in two days. The cursed Germans ensured that everything was on schedule.

The people were given different tasks. We put together a stove and a bathroom. Afterwards we went to work. A new leader arrived at the camp. The most senior was Kelerman. The senior work leader was an engineer named Bak. There was also a chief administrator. I did not know his name. We called him the screamer. He screamed but no one paid attention. There was another administrator who was calm and quiet. A third administrator was tall. We called him the "footballist" because he would always kick people.

The camp's labor force worked in two directions. One was toward Old Vilayke and the small city of Oshmyany, which was not far from the Oshmyany train station. The second direction was east, from Old Vilayke toward the Soviet Union, near the Oshmyany lodgings. We constructed a large workshop which was where we fixed all the tools that were needed for the tasks we performed. This was work for tool mechanics and I was a tool mechanic, so I was placed in the workshop. Ten Poles also worked there. Bak the engineer called me the master craftsman. I knew the craft better than the Poles. The engineer would from time to time reward me with a pack of cigarettes or a half a loaf of bread. These rewards had great value then.

It took six weeks to complete the job. After the work was finished, it was discovered that someone had stolen the hand drill, a tool we used from time to time to drill holes in thin steel. Who did the Poles accuse? They accused me. I was the person who stole it they said. Bak the engineer ordered me to return it by tomorrow. If I didn't give it back, I would be shot in the morning, he said. When I got back to camp, everybody knew what had happened. They were all sure that I would be shot in the morning.

OLD VILAYKE (Old Vileyka) is a town located in the Minsk region of Belarus, 160 kilometers north of Baranovich and 96 kilometers east of Vilna. The Nazi camp, which had previously been a Soviet prison camp, existed between August 1942 and July 1943.

Baruch Kudewicky, a former inmate, described the camp: "The Wilejka (Vilayke) camp was a labor camp, which was located approximately 100 meters from the train station. The camp consisted of a single barrack, which had been divided up into four rooms. One hundred people lived in each room. The camp was cordoned off with barbed wire, and was under constant guard of SS troops. Among the 400 men in the camp, there were also 23 women. All the camp inmates were young, healthy people, up to the age of forty. Most of them were Jews. Three hundred of these people were from Baranovich.... The SS were the overseers of the camp, but the work was directed by the people from the Todt Organization. The work consisted of building a railroad line, fifty kilometers in length, between Molodechno and Braslau. The inmates of the Wilejka camp worked on one side of the line, and the inmates from Stragy (a camp made up of 250 slave laborers) worked on the other side."[11]

Abraham Mazurek was a Jew who came from Warsaw. He, his wife and two children had been living in the Baranovich ghetto. He let it be known that he was a lawyer. Yankelewicz, the ghetto's elder, appointed Mazurek as his replacement. When they split us up in Old Vilayke, he accompanied the 300 people on their journey. I did not know the senior leader in the group of 700. When Mazurek was told that I would be shot in the morning, he visited me in the barracks. He told me that he would send two people to Oshmyany and maybe they would be able to buy another **drill**.

"You will then replace the new one for the old one."

I said that I would not accede to his recommendation: "Even if you do buy a new one and I replace the old one, they will accuse me of stealing. Then Bak will surely shoot me for stealing."

In the morning, when I went to work with the rest of the workers, they showed pity for me; they were seeing me for the last time. I could have escaped, but if I did, they would have shot twenty other workers. This was the policy of Hitler's regime.

We came to work at 8:00 A.M. Bak, the engineer, would arrive at 9:00 A.M. This morning he came in at 8:00. He entered the door of the workshop. He wanted to see me. He asked me if I would return the drill. I answered him: "I didn't take it and therefore I cannot return it." From the expression on his face I had the impression that he was going to shoot me. I had the power to tear him apart. I was young, healthy, and strong. Logic dictated that I should not do it. We Jews were destined to die and I would die one day. If I had killed him they would have killed twenty Jews. Then the engineer told me to go out and stand against the wall. I stood with my face to the wall. Then he told me to turn my face to him. He took out his revolver. At that moment the calm and quiet administrator approached him. He grabbed him by the hand and called him by his surname, "Bak!" he said, "If you harm him you will have committed a terrible deed. He is happy to work at our shop. He has food to eat. He did not steal the machine." He renounced his right to shoot me.

The engineer then called out to me, "Go to your job." Two large tears fell from both my eyes and I entered the workshop. I couldn't work because of

The importance of a DRILL can be seen in the following case. In the Ninth Fort [see note on the Ninth Fort in "A New Captain," chapter 8], known as the Death Fort, a small drill from the locksmith shop was smuggled into the prison cells where the inmates slept. It was used to make holes in the metal partition of the prison cells. The men then used a file to cut the steel between the holes and create an opening large enough for a man to pass through. In this way, twenty-three people escaped from the Death Fort on Christmas Day, 1943.[12]

my shaking hands. A pair of good-natured Poles offered me a cigarette and comforted me. When we returned to the barracks everyone was elated that I was still alive. Mazurek agreed with me that my response had been the correct one. He was very proud of me. After that, the workload returned to normal.

A few weeks passed, and two Poles got involved in a heated argument. It became so intense that they started fighting. Then one of them shouted out, "You stole the drill and sold it to a farmer for a liter of whiskey. They could have killed Abrashe." The engineer was informed of this incident. He called the SS. They came in one car and removed the thief. They investigated the allegations and concluded that the Pole and farmer were guilty, and shot them both. The engineer was now friendlier than before. The quiet and calm administrator came over to me. He took me aside and took out a red star. The soldiers of the Red Army wore this star on their hats. "Now you know who I am. You should also know that as long as I am here, no one will harm you and you shouldn't fear anybody."*

---

* TWO CAMPS: Baruch Kudewicky, an inmate at the Old-Vilayke camp, does not mention Abraham Mazurek as the *Ober Jude*, or Mazurek's having been sent by Yankelyevitsh of the Baranovich Judenrat. Kudewicky does not make a distinction between the group of 300 and the group of 700. To Kudewicky, there were only 400 inmates at Old-Vilayke, 300 of which came from Baranovich, housed in a "single, large barrack...divided into four rooms." But Abrashe above notes: "I was among a group of 300 people. We walked 10 kilometers further east of Old Vilayke. Here we had to build a barrack." Separating the two accounts further, Szabrinski also states that he did not know the senior person from the 700 but names Mazurek as the senior person of his group, while Kudewicky names Yankl Goldberg as *Ober Jude*. Also, in his testimony to Yad Vashem (see p. 142) Abrashe cites a New and an Old Vilayke. The two men are describing different camps, and Kudewicky gives evidence for a second camp when he mentions a camp called Stragy made up of 250 "slave laborers." How he distinguishes "slave labor" in this instance is unclear, but what this shows is there was more than one camp near Old-Vilayke. Furthermore, Kudewicky does show a possible avenue for Baranovich to have sent a leader as Abrashe stated happened. Kudewicky writes that "thanks to the efforts of the *Ober Jude*, a delegation of camp inmates traveled to Baranovich on two occasions..." This statement by Kudewicky simply shows that there was a living link between Baranovich and Old-Vilayke, a connection not uncommon at the time which also will occur between Vilna and its surrounding work camps. The two witnesses describe different endings for the camp. Kudewicky states that in July 1943 "the camp was liquidated and all the inmates were exterminated to the last one." In contrast, Abrashe in the following chapter explains that after typhus had struck the large camp the remaining inmates were liquidated, and the smaller camp was sent by train to Bezdani to work under the German jurisdiction of Vilna. See Baruch Kudewicky, "Uprising in the Old-Wilejka Camp," *Baranovich in Martyrdom & Resistance*, ed. Joseph Foxman (New York: The Baranovich Society for America, 1964), pp. 17–20; printed in *Baranovich the Trilogy*, ed. and trans. Jacob Solomon Berger (Mahwah, NJ, 2012).

Chapter 4

"And the Sabeans fell upon them, and took them away; yea, they have slain the servants with the edge of the sword; and I only am escaped alone to tell thee."

Job 1:15

Two Camps

What happened with the two camps? One camp was located in Vilayke and it had a population of 700 – Jews from Baranovich and **Byezshintes**. The Jewish Byezshintes came to Baranovich to escape the German occupation. A typhus epidemic broke out in this camp. Many people died because of it and the Germans killed those who survived. We worked for another month after that.

After the inmates of the large camp perished, Mazurek, the senior Jew of the smaller camp, befriended Kelerman, the German head of the camp. Mazurek would collect money and gold that the Jews kept in their clothing and give it to Kelerman, who allowed Mazurek **freedom of movement**. This was why Mazurek would often travel to the city of Oshmyany.

Our camp was not far from Oshmyany and came under the Vilna jurisdiction. Kelerman devised a plan together with the leader of the Vilna Commissariat area. Kelerman explained that "The workers of our camp are an excellent work force. It would be extremely

BYEZSHINTES

Earlier (chapters 1 and 2), Abrashe explained that Byezshintes were refugees from the other side of the Bug River where the Germans ruled. As he himself swam across river, and was not from Baranovich, but Seltz, it's difficult to understand the distinction he is making between himself and Byezshintes, except that since he was in the Red Army, he was not viewed, nor did he view himself as a refugee but as a soldier. Apparently, Byezshintes were taken in by various charities that operated in Baranovich before the Nazis invaded. Dr. Sh. Klass estimates that of 12,000 Jews in Baranovich at the time of invasion, 3,000 were refugees from western Poland.[1] In his book *Scrolls of Testimony*, Abba Kovner calls the refugees *Bjezenczi*.[2]

FREEDOM OF MOVEMENT

Bribery was not uncommon under the system of exploitation and murder imposed by Nazi Germany. And while allowing Jews freedom of movement in return for money does not at first appear to be a likely scenario, Kudewicky in his short memoir mentions that in the Old Vilayke camp, the *Ober Jude* paid ten thousand Soviet rubles for "permission to travel to Baranovich" to procure food and clothing for the inmates. Also, stealing from Jews was Nazi policy, and the line between theft, bribery, and a licensing fee was purposely vague.[3]

advantageous for Vilna if they would allow us in its area. We should be allowed to organize a work camp in Vilna."

Mazurek acquainted himself with the underground organizations that had contacts with people in the forest and his name was given to the partisans in White Russian forests. One day, when Mazurek was returning from Oshmyany, I came to him with a proposal. "We should all go to the **forest**," I said. He asked me, "What will happen to the elderly and infirmed of our group?" I replied, "In order to save 280 we must be ready to sacrifice twenty." He knew I was right. "I will inform you when that time will be," he said.

Escape from the ghettos to the **FOREST** was extremely difficult and complicated. Not only were reprisals from the Germans swift and severe, but they were aimed mainly at the family, friends, and in many cases the neighbors of the escapees. Neither was the forest a welcome environment for Jews. The Russian and Polish partisans who inhabited these forests were notoriously anti-Semitic and of a murderous disposition.

In his account of the Baranovich liquidation, Dr. Levin book recalls that "Some escapees are murdered by the Germans and also by partisan bandit groups on the way to the forest such as…Dr. Avrasheh Abramowsky…. The partisans [took] note of his new boots, and his good warm clothes, as well as his revolver. They [took] all this away from him and [shot] him."[4]

In the camp, one third of the group agreed with me. I felt that the work assignment was coming to an end and that death was very near. Within a week, Mazurek suddenly disappeared. We ran to the camp's senior official and he told us that Mazurek would not return. He also told us that in two days our camp was being relocated to an area close to Vilna that would be our new workplace.

In our camp there were many types of individuals. The most respected was Aharon Slutsky. He was short, slightly built, and in his forties. He came from a wealthy Baranovich family, and before the war he had also been the editor of the Baranovich newspaper. His brother-in-law, Brod, came from Warsaw. He had married Aharon's only sister when she was already not a young woman. Slutsky introduced himself as a former medical student from Warsaw, whose studies had been suspended because of the war.

Kelerman ordered the camp to choose new leaders. Slutsky and his brother-in-law Brod were selected as the representatives, as was Kulyasky from the old leadership. They were responsible for keeping order in the camp. They wanted me to be Brod's deputy, but I didn't want to be chosen for any office in the camp. They knew my position concerning escape to the forest. When Mazurek was with us, Slutsky would explain the correctness of my proposal to him. I was the oldest man in barracks no. 1. There were four barracks that housed seventy-five men each. We were all friendly and shared the same ideal.

Three days passed, then, on the fourth day, we were ordered to assemble and get ready to travel in one transport from the railroad station of Oshmyany. From there we would move on in the direction of Vilna. Our camp was apportioned seven cars. In Vilna we were to change to another train that would take us to our new camp. The procedure of changing trains did not take very long.

One thousand people were being transferred to this work camp. The guards assigned to transport us were Lithuanians. They were devoted to the Germans. All the transports left at the designated time. The Nazis were very punctual in everything they did. We organized ourselves while we were being transported to Vilna and decided that if we were to be taken to some place other than Vilna, we would flee for our lives.

We arrived in Vilna, changed to another train, and then traveled in an easterly direction. After we entered the station, they told us to disembark. From there we had to walk two kilometers to a camp called **Bezdani**. This area was 20 kilometers from Vilna. The camp had large barracks and a few standard homes that were not very big. We were housed in the barracks during the time of our work assignment. The administrators of the camp were quartered in the small houses. The work consisted of digging up turf – black earth that was dried and then used for fuel.

BEZDANI was a forced labor camp located east of Vilna. In his book *Ghetto in Flames*, Dr. Yitzhak Arad writes about this camp and the work done there. "The peat digging camps had been created at the beginning of the German occupation, and in the summer of 1942 they were increased...." The camp was completely destroyed in July 1943.[5]

The camp was situated in a forest surrounded by giant trees. When we finally started settling down, I was approached by our representative, Aharon Slutsky. He said, "Avraham. You wanted the forest and now we're in the forest."

I replied, "What is the name of the place?"

He answered, "Bezdani." In the camp it was referred to as *biz danen* [which means "up to here" in Yiddish].

As I understood the situation, the work was a farce. We had been brought here temporarily. Something did not add up, but I did not know what it was nor did I comprehend what was happening. Full order was established in camp. The senior member of the camp was a Pole named Mankevitsh. The guards were Lithuanians. The camp ran with complete discipline. About 200 men went out to work, while the rest had jobs in the camp itself. They were cooks, tailors, shoemakers, and did various other tasks connected to camp life. We also had a doctor who came from Grodno. Brod, the leader of the camp, and his deputy Aharon Slutsky, as well as Kulyasky, the leader of the Jewish guards, were all punctual in their actions. Mankevitsh the Pole was in charge of community relations. Slutsky informed me that the food supplies were ordered by the Vilna ghetto administration. Our camp was considered part of the Vilna ghetto, along with other camps that were in the Vilna area and under the jurisdiction of the Vilna commissariat.

Dr. Zelik Levinbook mentions that **MAZUREK** was shot by the partisans in the forest as an English spy. The partisans were as quick to shoot someone they suspected of being a spy as they were to shoot someone for breach of protocol.[6]

In the camp we often heard news from the front. We were informed that **Mazurek**, who had been the elder of our camp, had escaped to the woods. He fled with members of the underground from Oshmyany. When he met up with the partisans, they put him on trial. They felt that since he was the elder of the group, he was its captain. A captain does not leave his ship, therefore, they ruled that he had not done his duty and they shot him. It was my opinion that he deserved this end. I proposed to him, as I have previously written, that we should escape to the forest. He did not want to hear of it at a time that had been most ripe for escaping and meeting up with the partisans.

PONARY

The name itself came to mean death for the Jews of Vilna and many other ghettos. The Russians had begun digging large trenches on this site for the mass storage of oil. The Nazis invaded before the work could be completed and the Germans found the location suitable for their murderous aims. As many as 60,000 people were shot to death here between July 1941 and August 1944.[7]

THE BANDITS

The labor camps outside Vilna were destroyed starting in the end of June 1943. The destruction of Bezdani began on July 9, according to Yitzhak Arad. As Abrashe suspected, the arrival of the officer in charge of the Security Police, **BRUNO KITELL**, heralded the end. According to Dr. Arad, Kitell ordered the workers to assemble in a warehouse. He announced that it was "the duty of the camp inmates to work, not to be in touch with 'men of the forests' or engage in smuggling." He accused them of having connections with the partisans, which they did, and this was the reason they were being annihilated. While Kitell was talking, members of the Security Police, as well as Lithuanians, assembled outside the building, or the barbed wire fence. When he had finished speaking and left the building, these murderers opened fire and threw grenades inside. Kitell had exterminated the Kena camp in the same way the day before.[9]

We also found out that the transport we had been on had been carrying Jews from a certain shtetl. They were taken to **Ponary**, not far from Vilna, where they were shot. Jews and Christians in the Vilna train station told us that the victims had been coming from the east, from the Soviet Union, and asking about the city of Ponary. They did not know that death was on the horizon. This was what was happening. This was the work of Hitler's murder machine.

We performed unimportant tasks until July 13, 1943. On that day, two well-known "**bandits**" of Vilna came to our camp. One was

Bruno Kitell and the other **Martin Weiss**. They ordered all the workers to leave their work stations and go to the large plaza surrounded by barbed wire, where they could be seen. The Germans wanted to count the camp population. Outside the barbed wire perimeter, Lithuanian guards also watched us. These guards were real bandits.

We couldn't leave by way of the gate. To escape, we had to enter the barracks and jump to the other side. Next to me stood a young man from Baranovich whose name was Ize Svayatitski. I said to him, "Let's escape because this is the end." He replied, "Don't be silly, they're only going to count us." I did not listen to him and ran into the barracks. I jumped through an open window to the other side of the camp and ran deeper into the forest.

MARTIN WEISS was a sergeant major in the SS, and de facto Nazi overseer of the Vilna ghetto. He was also chief of the Ipatinga, or Lithuanian Einsatzgruppen, responsible for many of the murders inside Vilna and at the mass murder site Ponary. He was among the most feared of all the Nazis in Vilna. Sutskever recounts that he took the hand of a twelve-year-old girl who was not wearing the yellow star. She felt comforted by him. Then he put her against a wall and shot her. He also invented a typhus epidemic and murdered the children whose mothers had brought them in for innoculation.[10]

BRUNO KITELL

"Kitell, born in Austria, had been a film actor and vocalist before the outbreak of the war. After joining the Security Police, he dealt with Jewish affairs in France and Riga, Latvia, and then went to Vilna. He was dubbed, *ex post facto*, the 'liquidator of the Vilna ghetto.'"[8]

There I met a young boy from our camp by the name of Nokhke Byalistatski. He had arrived late for the count. Nokhke and I began our trek, walking through sown cornfields in the direction of Vilna. We arrived in Bey Vilayke, which was one kilometer from Vilna. At the Bey Vilayke train station, we met the Jews from Vilna who worked there.

The settlement leader was a young man named Yisraeleyk. He advised us to hide under the wagons. He also told us to pretend that we were workers. "In a few hours we will go to **Vilna** and you will accompany us."

In *Ghetto in Flames*, Yitzhak Arad mentions that massacres outside of **VILNA**, including those in the labor camps, stimulated a large increase in underground activity and sent hundreds of young men into Vilna. Many of them had connections either with those already in the forests or with the local peasantry. The presence of these young men (men like Abrashe) in Vilna helped bring about a larger exodus from the ghetto to the forest.[11] Thus Abrashe's arrival in Vilna at this time would have already been anticipated by both the ghetto police and the partisans. These two groups had an overlapping and antagonistic relationship.

Chapter 5

"Brothers, it is better to die as free fighters than to live at the mercy of killers. Resist, resist, to our last breath."[1]

Abba Kovner

"I calculate the price of Jewish blood and not Jewish honor. If I am asked for 1,000 Jews I deliver them. For if we Jews do not deliver them, the Germans will come and take them by force and then it will not be a question of 1,000 but of thousands and the entire ghetto will perish."[2]

Jacob Gens

The Ghetto Gate

And so it was. We had good fortune and everything went well for us. When we reached the gate of the Vilna ghetto, the Jewish policemen stopped us. They led us to the police office at the gate. The Vilna police knew that *Aktions* were taking place in the work camps in the surrounding areas. It became known to me later that there was an agreement between **Gens,** the commandant of the Vilna ghetto, the frightful informer and traitor **Dessler,** and **Murer,** the Nazi bandit. If and when the Nazis demanded Jews, the Judenrat would instead offer those who were in the camps around Vilna. Gens wanted to push off the decree that would uproot the Jews of Vilna for as long as he could. He had the fantasy that a great miracle was about to happen.

JACOB GENS was the head of the Jewish ghetto police in Vilna and later the "ghetto representative," the sole head of the Vilna ghetto working under the direction of the Gestapo. He believed that he could lead the remnant of Lithuanian Jewry out of the nightmare of the Holocaust. Gens explained this belief in August 1943: "I want to postpone the *Aktion* so as to gain time, which is so valuable for us. Time is on our side. I am convinced that the Soviet Army will reach Vilna by December of this year, and if at that time the ghetto still survives, even though a few will be left in it, I shall know that I completed my task. I can then announce with a quiet heart and pure conscience that I did my duty to my people and to the future. Jews, try to hold on until the end and believe that we shall win a better life."[3]

Ultimately, he failed. Almost all the Jews of Vilna were murdered. Gens himself was shot in the middle of September 1943. His murder heralded the end of the Vilna ghetto.[4] Gens could have escaped internment in Vilna but he chose not to. In fact, according to Joseph Harmatz, Gens's wife and daughter lived outside the ghetto.[5] When he learned the Nazis were going to execute him, Gens did not flee as he could have because he believed his death would cause more pain for the ghetto.[6]

SALEK DESSLER was a feared and hated member of the Jewish ghetto police. When Gens was made "ghetto representative," Dessler was made chief of police, and when Gens was murdered Dessler fled.[7] Isaac Kowalski writes that during one *Aktion*, Dessler sold "life passes" to the highest bidder for "thousands of marks."[8]

FRANZ MURER

Isaac Kowalski called him the "hangman of Vilna."[9] He was an SS officer known as the "Jewish expert," who oversaw the Vilna ghetto.[10]

31

He believed that the Jews of Vilna would be saved from annihilation. But this was an absurd thought.

When the guards at the gate detained Nokhke and me, a guest greeted us. He was **Solomon Gens**, brother of the ghetto commandant. He had the rank of commissar. He was a good person. I never heard anybody speak ill of him. Accompanying him was Commissar Berenshteyn. He was an awful person. Also with them was a young individual in civilian clothing. I asked him his name. He told me that his name was Lyevos and he was a commandant of the Jewish gate patrol. I asked why he didn't have patches on his jacket, since every Jew was forced to wear a yellow patch. He said that he was an exception. He had permission to go wherever he wanted to without a yellow patch. I told him that he would receive two bullets from the Nazis instead of one.

They questioned us about everything that had happened at the Bezdani camp. I told them everything. They informed me that a few camps around Vilna had been destroyed. They also said that disguised Lithuanians and Germans had been stationed on the other side of the Bezdani camp. They entered the camp, and instead of taking a census, shot everyone. They burned all the barracks. This was the end of the Bezdani camp. This took place on July 13, 1943.

They kept Nokhke and me in the ghetto guardhouse for two days. They told us that this was for our own security. They brought us food and even a little bottle of whiskey. Many different policemen came to interrogate us. One of them impressed me as being a smart young man. His name was **Joseph Harmatz**. He was one of the good ones. I was able to trust him and speak earnestly to him. I said to him, "Herr Yolik," this was what they called him in the ghetto. "Is there an underground organization in the forest? Yes or no? If there is, I want to contact them and join their organization. If not, then

SOLOMON GENS was Jacob's brother and a member of the Judenrat. He later became part of the ghetto police. After his brother's murder he was elected by Kitell as a member of the new Judenrat. Isaac Kowalski in his *A Secret Press in Nazi Europe*, recalls that on September 1, 1943, Solomon helped lead a unit of SS through a side entrance where they attacked a group of partisans. He was certainly not uncontroversial.[11]

JOSEPH HARMATZ was born in Rokishkis, Lithuania, and his family moved to Vilna in 1940 just ahead of the Nazis. His father went to a friend's house one evening, and when he did not return, Joseph went there. He was handed a note his father had left. It said: "My dear ones: we are living through difficult times; I can find no way to endure this kind of existence. I am sorry. I am withdrawing from life. Be well." Joseph was a member of the Komsomol, the communist youth movement, and the Nazis and their collaborators were hunting for him personally from the earliest days of the occupation of Vilna. But this membership allowed him access to the FPO, which was an "all-party" organization drawing mostly from the young and politically active Jewish population. Eventually, Harmatz escaped through the sewers with the partisans and fought in the forests with Abrashe. After the war, Harmatz took part in a plot to poison the German water supply, and ultimately poisoned loaves of bread given to SS POWs. He moved to Israel.[12]

I have nothing to do here. My entire focus is on being in the forest. I am a professional and schooled soldier. I served in the Polish army and in the Russian army."

"I will answer you in the morning." In the morning he came to see me and said, "She told me that you will be part of our unit, and I will be your mentor for all matters. You will be part of my unit, the Finftl." I asked who the *she* was that he was referring to. Later on I found out that the woman was **Khyene Borowska,** a communist who later became our commissar with responsibility over Jewish affairs in the forest.

In July 1943, there were 20,000 people in the Vilna ghetto. Before Hitler's occupation of Lithuania 60,000 Jews had been living in the city. Along with those who had come from other cities, Vilna's Jewish population added up to 70,000. The murderous German plan of destruction was excellent and pinpointed. As the Nazis' actions were meticulous, the Jews were naïvely hoping for the great miracle. For a long time the Jews of Vilna and other cities did not believe that the Germans wanted to annihilate them. There were many opportunities to save Jews, thousands of Jews, and maybe even tens of thousands of Jews.

In the beginning, the Jewish leaders of the ghettos had had all the right intentions. As time went by, they were fooled by the craftiness of the devil and they had no way out. This happened to **Rumkowski** in Lodz as well as Gens in Vilna, and who knows how many more of these situations repeated themselves, let alone how the leaders were fooled into the death camps. In the Vilna ghetto and other ghettos with a considerable number of people, the Jews organized underground units. They in turn joined the Soviet partisans in different forests. In Vilna, with the assistance of the underground, the Jews established a partisan organization called the **FPO**, an acronym that

KHYENE BOROWSKA

Originally from Vilna, Borowska had first been a member of the socialist Zionist youth movement Hashomer Hatza'ir and later became a communist. She was one of the founders of the FPO in Vilna, which was open to members of all political movements.[13]

CHAIM RUMKOWSKI was elected "Elder Jew" by the Nazis in the city of Lodz, Poland. Like Gens, he worked with the Nazis to organize the ghetto and believed that Jewish labor would keep the city's Jews alive. He was on the last train to Auschwitz and was murdered there in August 1944.[14]

FPO

The FPO was founded in Vilna on January 21, 1942, in the home of Joseph Glazman expressly for the purpose of armed combat. It was the first Jewish resistance group to be formed during the Holocaust and the first to comprehend the Nazi plans for extermination. The FPO made attempts to contact other ghettos and inform the people there about what was happening. Vilna was not the first ghetto to witness murder, but it was the first large ghetto where mass exterminations of the Jews took place. The group also published anti-Nazi propaganda and counterfeited various official Nazi documents, using the printing press that Isaac Kowalski had stolen piece by piece and then assembled in the ghetto. The FPO issued a call to arms titled "The First Call," which was written by the poet and fighter Abba Kovner. During the liquidation of the Vilna Ghetto, as popular resistance failed to materialize, the FPO with some 80 members escaped through the sewers and into the nearby Rudnicki forest, where they established contact with the Russian Partisans. Many FPO members, including Abrashe, lived to retake Vilna alongside their Russian compatriots.[15]

stood for *Fareynegte Partizaner Organizatsye* (United Partisan Organization). Its top leader in the ghetto was Isaac Wittenberg. He was a quilter by profession and a member of the Communist Party. His closest associates were Khyene Borowska, also a member of the Communist Party; **Shmuel Kaplinski**, a member of the Bund and a cleaner by trade; **Abba Kovner**, a poet and member of Hashomer Hatza'ir, and others.

The **Rudnicki Forest** was located thirty kilometers from Vilna. It was a large forest measuring about 2,500 square kilometers [see note on the Rudnicki Forest in "An Attack on a German Convoy," chapter 9] and there were few villages in that area. Before the war, the Polish leader Joseph Pilsudski vacationed in this forest together with Hitler's Marshal Goring. They would come to hunt. One unfortunate aspect of the forest was that a highway running from Lida to Vilna passed through it. In 1942, there were already partisan groups in the Rudnicki Forest. Some were Soviet expatriates and others had escaped from German prisons.

The Vilna leadership did little to assist the young men and women to escape into the forest. There were many opportunities to do so, but the leaders of the underground tarried. They believed the advice of the ghetto leadership; however, those leaders were not realistic with their evaluations, therefore **misleading the youth** of the ghetto. Many young people could have been saved from death. They could have escaped into the Rudnicki Forest, which was a mere thirty kilometers from Vilna. There were many opportunities and they had the means to accomplish this.

During the liquidation of the camps

SHMUEL KAPLINSKI worked in a factory in the ghetto repairing broken firearms and making other weapons. Whenever possible, he smuggled these weapons out of the factory, helping to build the anti-Nazi arsenal for the FPO. He was also instrumental in mapping the Vilna sewers and leading the FPO out of the ghetto.[16]

ABBA KOVNER was a leading activist in the socialist Zionist youth movement, Hashomer Hatza'ir. When the Nazis overtook Lithuania, he was able to hide in a convent outside of Vilna. He was an integral part in the founding of the FPO, and wrote "The First Call," which is probably most famous for the line, "Let us not go like sheep to the slaughter." He escaped with the FPO under his command and fought in the forests with the Russian partisans.[17]

The partisan base in the **RUDNICKI FOREST** camp was in fact built around an old hunting lodge established by the Polish royal family.[18]

MISLEADING THE YOUTH

This is an important criticism of the FPO in Vilna, and was a question they themselves often debated. Abrashe was in a unique position to criticize. After he saw what happened in Baranovich, Old Vilayke, and Bezdani, he had no illusions about what the Nazis were doing. Abba Kovner, too, harbored no illusions, but he had been a founding member of the FPO, which had been created to revolt from within the ghetto. Neither revolt nor escape was viable. In Warsaw, the uprising had in fact led to the ghetto's immediate liquidation. Nor was mass escape possible, and if only FPO members escaped, then the murderous reprisal by the Nazis against the rest of the Jews would have been horrendous. In the end, the ghetto was liquidated and the FPO did escape, leaving family members and loved ones to their fate.[19]

around Vilna, a great catastrophe occurred. The Gestapo arrested a certain Pole by the name of Kozlowski. He was a member of the partisan municipal committee. He was severely tortured and divulged the name of Isaac Wittenberg, the commandant of the partisans in the Vilna ghetto. Everyone understood that the organization had been compromised and was now unmasked. Kitell, the brutal and murderous one, demanded that Gens hand Wittenberg over alive.

Wittenberg did not volunteer to surrender to the Gestapo and in my opinion he was correct. His friends in the persons of Khyene Borowska from the communists, Abba Kovner of Hashomer Hatza'ir, Yehiel Shaynboym of Hehalutz, Nissan Reznik of Hanoar Hatzioni, and the chairman of the Revisionists (I do not know his name), and surely Gens and Dessler pressured him and talked to him incessantly about giving himself up to Kitell, alive. They did him a brotherly favor by giving him poison. He would take the poison if and when his torture became unbearable. In the end he swallowed the poison. This was one of the dirtiest and lowest deeds that comrades could have possibly perpetrated against the commandant of the partisans of the Vilna ghetto. Their excuse was that with his death, the ghetto would be saved from immediate destruction. This notion was silly and quite absurd since so many Jews had already been murdered in Vilna. Jews still held this notion even knowing the reality of the situation. Soon after **the death of Wittenberg**, Kitell shot **Gens**, and then Dessler fled the ghetto with his blond witch, his wife who was more than ten times as bad as her traitor husband (that was how the Jews of the Vilna ghetto spoke of

THE DEATH OF WITTENBERG

On July 8, Kitell went to the ghetto and demanded that Gens hand over Wittenberg. On July 15, Gens in turn asked the FPO leadership to come to his house for a meeting. When Kovner, Borowska, and Wittenberg arrived, Dessler and some ghetto police arrested him. Outside, however, Kaplinski and a group of FPO attacked the ghetto police and the Lithuanians holding Wittenberg and freed him. When Gens could not hand over Wittenberg, Kitell threatened to liquidate the ghetto. The people were horrified. Again, the FPO leadership met with Gens, who convinced them to turn Wittenberg in. They told Wittenberg that if he gave the order they would begin open warfare. But when he learned that the communist group was for his surrender, and that the people of the ghetto also desired it, he turned himself in. On July 16, Wittenberg presented himself to Gens and Dessler. According to Arad, Gens told him that if he made it through the first day of interrogation, he (Gens) would have him freed. In case he could not hold out, Gens gave him arsenic. The following morning, Wittenberg was found dead from poisoning. This affair sums up the ghetto's dilemma: should all be jeopardized for the sake of one?[20]

On September 14, 1943, the Nazi Security Police summoned Jacob GENS to their headquarters. Gens had been warned the previous day by Weiss that he would be executed.[21] Despite this warning, he went knowingly to his death. He said that if he fled, it would bring a "calamity to the entire ghetto." He left his brother at the gate. He explained that if Solomon did not see him by 8:00 PM then he would never return. Both Jacob Gens and Salek Dessler went to the Security Police Headquarters. Dessler was sent back, but Gens was taken and held. Obersturmführer Neuegebauer and Weiss then took Gens into the courtyard of the headquarters, where a grave had already been dug. Gens was blindfolded and shot.[21]

them).* They hid in a hiding place outside the ghetto that had previously been prepared.

The ghetto was closed. No one could enter or leave it. Everyone understood that the end was near. Groups began escaping to the forest. Isolated groups encountered Germans and **Lithuanians** who were guarding the escape routes. A lot of young men and women **lost their lives**. The majority of them did everything they could to reach the forest. Certain groups went as far as the thick forests of White Russia, a distance of 200 kilometers. From this we can conclude and be convinced of the confusion of our leadership. They worked in the dark. The Rudnicki Forest was only thirty kilometers from Vilna, but instead they sent people 200 kilometers away. They were endangering their lives with such an odyssey not to mention their ammunition.

Jacob Gens

Jacob Gens was a Lithuanian Jew from the city of Kovno. He was a handsome man. He married a Lithuanian Christian woman. They had one daughter. I believe that after the war, the wife and daughter went to America. Before the war he was

LITHUANIANS

An insight into many Lithuanians' sentiments toward Jews can be gleaned from a statement published by the Lithuanian Activists Front (LAF) just prior to the German invasion. It reads, in part, "The crucial day of reckoning has come for the Jews at last. Lithuania must be liberated not only from the Asiatic Bolshevik slavery but also from the Jewish yoke of long standing."[22]

LOST THEIR LIVES

On July 24, a group of twenty-one FPO members left for the Narocz Forest situated some 241 kilometers from Vilna. On the way, the group, known as the Leon Group after Wittenberg's code name, was joined by a group of fourteen from a labor camp outside the ghetto. The Leon Group agreed to take these men and women with them. But on a bridge crossing the Vilayke River, some 32 kilometers from Vilna, the group was ambushed by Nazis and nine FPO men lost their lives. This group was sent to the Narocz Forest at the request of Markov, a Russian partisan commander. Gens knew about this mission but did nothing to stop it. When the FPO prepared for its final escape, Yurgis [see note on Yurgis in "The Forest," chapter 7] finally sent the order for them to go to the Rudnicki Forest rather than far-off Narocz.[23]

* See Balberyszski, Mendel, *Stronger Than Iron* (Jerusalem: Gefen, 2010), p. 257. "On September 18, at 2:00 pm, the ghetto had a new sensation: Salek Dessler, the man who had acted as the supreme contact between the ghetto and the Gestapo, had run away together with his wife. Detailed information reached us that Dessler's wife had left the ghetto with a small suitcase in her hand and her husband followed soon after. Sources at the office of the Judenrat informed us that before fleeing, Dessler removed from the Judenrat safe many thousands of rubles in gold and diamonds." The Desslers were not the only leaders to leave the ghetto, as Balberyszski further recounts. "A number of people who had ruled the ghetto with their iron fists for two years also ran away.... During the last few nights, groups of young people also left the ghetto to join the partisans in the forests...but for the rest of us, numbering about twelve thousand people, there was no escape.... In the leaderless ghetto everything became surreal."

a member of **Brith Hahayal**, which was part of the Revisionist Party. Gens
was a captain in the Lithuanian army. He had
a brother, Solomon, who was also in the Vilna
ghetto and like him, served as a policeman.
They had an old mother. Every Friday she
would bless the Sabbath candles. It was common knowledge that she was eighty years old.
I was in the Vilna ghetto for two months and
never saw her once. Gens had the opportunity
to be hidden by any of his many Lithuanian
friends as well as his wife's family. Thereby he
would have escaped the torture of war, but instead he went with the other
Jews into the Vilna ghetto.

    In order to understand the reasons we must, with truthfulness, understand
the situation that we all found ourselves in. Not only Gens, but also many
Jews did not believe that we were all sentenced
to death. Gens believed he could play an important role in the Jewish community and be
a liaison with the Germans. Why? He was a
charismatic person with a military ego and had
hundreds of friends in the Lithuanian community. Since these friends were outspoken na-
tionalists who worked with the Germans, he
thought he could succeed in Jewish matters
while others failed. He would then become the
most important Jew of those tragic times. In
reality, he deceived himself. When I heard his
last **speech** from the balcony of the Judenrat
office, I felt that it was very profound. He said
that if he could successfully rescue thousands
of Jews from the ghetto, he would consider
himself a very fortunate individual. He would
then agree to be judged by a "folks" court. He
knew that his hands were tainted with Jewish
blood. This indeed was so. He had gone into

BRITH HAHAYAL was a right-wing, paramilitary Zionist organization that had become influential in the
years prior to the war. However, Gens's membership
in this group is complicated as he was also a devout
Lithuanian nationalist. N.N. Shneidman, who wrote a
short biography of Gens, comments that "As a native
of Lithuania, and a Jew, he (Gens) believed that he
had an obligation to serve both the interests of his
native country, as well as the national cause of the
Jewish people. In both instances, his main interest
and contribution was mainly of a military nature. The
Zionism of Gens was ideological rather than national,
and he never intended to move to Palestine."[24]

Defending himself, Gens gave the following **SPEECH**:
"I, Gens, lead you to your death; and I, Gens, want to
save Jews from death. I, Gens, order hideouts to be
blown up; and I, Gens, do all in my power to create
work certificates, employment, and anything that
serves the ghetto. I calculate the price of Jewish blood
and not Jewish honor. If I am asked for 1,000 Jews
I deliver them. For if we Jews do not deliver them,
the Germans will come and take them by force and
then it will not be a question of 1,000 but of thousands and the entire ghetto will perish. By delivering
hundreds I save thousands and by delivering 1,000
I save 10,000. You are the men of intellect and the
pen. You are not dealing with the filth of the ghetto.
You will come out clean from the ghetto. And if you
survive the ghetto you will say: 'we have come out
with clean consciences.' But if I, Gens, survive, I shall
come out soiled and with blood dripping from my
hands. And yet I shall present myself willingly to be
judged. To be judged by Jews. I will say: 'I did everything in my power to save as many Jews as possible
from the ghetto and lead them to freedom. And in
order that at least a remnant of Jews should survive,
I personally had to lead Jews to their deaths; and so
that some people should be able to leave the ghetto
with clean consciences, I had to wallow in filth and
act without conscience."[25]

the ghetto with good intentions, and Kitell shot him like an unfortunate Jew drawn into a web of bestial fascism. He had no avenue of escape.

Gens deserved to die, but not by German bullets, instead he deserved to die by Jewish bullets. When he shot a young man who had come from the forest to take fellow Jews back with him to the partisans, the Jewish organizations [the FPO] should have taken action against him right then and there. They should have killed Gens, Salek Dessler and his blond witch. The Jewish organizations should have behaved according to the standards to which they had pledged themselves. What do you think would have happened? Kitell would have assigned two other Jews as leaders of the Vilna ghetto. All the ghettos had been given a death sentence.

Vilna Police

I do not know how many **policemen** were in the ghetto. I believe there were a few hundred. They had various ranks. I knew many of them. They each had different personalities. There were good people and bad people, but in general they were divided into three groups. Fifty percent were idiots that followed the lead of Gens and Dessler; they looked upon them as their gods and worshipped them faithfully. Thirty to forty percent were sly individuals. They knew what would happen to the Jews and they felt that by being inside the system they and their families would be saved from death. Some of them were also part of the partisan movement. Many of them were able to save themselves from annihilation. Fifteen percent were traitors and informers – the greatest bastards of the Vilna ghetto. A great many were killed because their hands were **soaked in Jewish blood**. The policemen cleaned out whole villages of Jews, for example, **Sol and Oshmyany**. They tricked the Jews, telling them that they were being sent to the ghettos of Vilna or Kovno. In fact, they were taken to Ponary. They never told any of the youth that they should run

POLICEMEN

Several partisans were part of the Vilna ghetto's Jewish police force, among them Joseph Harmatz and Leizer Bart. Joseph Glazman, a Zionist Revisionist like Gens, was the deputy chief of the Jewish ghetto police. On one occasion, Glazman refused a direct order from Gens and was arrested, but the FPO rescued him from the hands of the ghetto police.[26]

SOAKED IN JEWISH BLOOD

"In the Lithuanian Central State Archive there is a list of forty-nine Jewish ghetto policemen who allegedly participated in criminal activities against the Jewish ghetto population. Six of them were shot by the Germans. Seven were shot by Soviet partisans. Some others managed to avoid Soviet retribution by escaping in time to Poland."[27]

for their lives. They carried out the work of the German devils, as the Germans would have done.

I wish I could put them on trial and shoot them. I would not make any mistakes. This is a correct evaluation of their deeds and no one can deny it.

SOL AND OSHMYANY were two of the villages that Gens and the Vilna ghetto police helped to organize onto trains in early April 1943 for liquidation. The Jews of these smaller ghettos were supposed to be sent to Vilna and Kovno. The first group of people was in fact sent to Vilna, but a later train, on which Gens himself was a passenger, was rerouted to Ponary and the people were all executed. According to Yitzhak Arad, Gens was tricked in this instance, but allowed to escape with his life. This incident was one of the indicators that the liquidation of Vilna was near, and one of the more egregious acts that Gens and his police perpetrated.[28]

The partisan Abrashe Szabrinski in liberated Vilnius (Vilna). He is holding a submachine gun.

Two Jewish partisans in liberated Vilnius (Vilna). In the photo: Abrashe Szabrinski (on the right) and Josef (Julek) Harmatz with Valentina Paszewelska. Photographed, evidently, in the summer of 1944. Photo from the estate of Yitzhak Alperovich.

A group of partisans in Lithuania, from the To Victory partisan battalion. Jewish partisan Abrashe Sz-abrinski served in this unit. Photo from the estate of Yitzhak Alperovich.

Three partisans in Lithuania. In the photo: Abrashe Szabrinski (center) and Lionka (Leon) Tshibuk (left). Tshibuk fell late in the war, in the battles for Berlin. Photo from the estate of Yitzhak Alperovich.

Abrashe Szabrinski, a Jewish soldier in the Polish army in 1938. Photographed in Torun. Photo from the estate of Yitzhak Alperovich.

A memorial assembly held in the Turkheim DP camp in Germany, 1947. In the photo: Abrashe Szabrinski (speaking). Photo from the estate of Yitzhak Alperovich.

The speakers' table at a conference of Revisionist Zionism for Holocaust refugees in postwar Germany. The conference was held in 1948 with the participation of Holocaust survivors in the western part of Germany. In the photo: Abrashe Szabrinski (center), the chairman and two members of the Betar movement (background). Photo from the estate of Yitzhak Alperovich.

VVGŽM.

Certificate issued to the leader of the Death to Fascists Unit, Abrashe Szabrinski

Joe Sabrin at monument to the partisans, Rudnicki Forest

Entrance to a partisan bunker, Rudnicki Forest, Vilnius, Lithuania (Vilna, Poland)

Joe Sabrin pointing to a photograph of his father at the Vilna Gaon Museum

Map of Vilna Ghetto, Vilna Gaon Museum

The Yiddish-language typewriter (made by *Olivetti*) used by Abrashe Szabrinski to write his memoirs

Chapter 6

"The orders were clear – only members of the underground were allowed to enter. The escape had to be kept secret from family members too. When I left, I left my younger brother Efraim and my mother behind."

Joseph Harmatz on escaping Vilna[1]

"We encountered an old farmer. I greeted him with a hearty 'good evening.' He was a smart and good man. If I were an observant and believing Jew, I would have thought that we met Elijah."

Abrashe Szabrinski

The Sewers

The liquidation of the Vilna ghetto began. The Nazis gathered all the Jews of the Vilna ghetto in a place called Rosa Square. The weak, the aged, and the sick were taken to Ponary. From Rosa Square, the young and the healthy Jews were sent to the train station and from there to concentration camps in Estonia. The **Vilna Jewish police** and their officers were in charge of this task. The Germans had complete trust in these people. The Jews were led to work centers that would eventually lead to their deaths. September 23, 1943, was the last day of the ghetto's existence. That morning, the leader of the FPO [Abba Kovner] decided that we should escape to the forest by way of the city sewers.

This plan had already been prepared on 12 Strashuna Street and disseminated among the FPO's members. To this end, they stored arms, bullets, and hand grenades. It was imperative that we divide up into small groups if we were to reach Rudnicki Street, where we would enter a cellar that would lead us to the sewers. In the sewers, we met a lot of

VILNA JEWISH POLICE

Mendel Balberyszski recounts that the ghetto police and members of the council organized Jews for the final trips to "work" camps in Estonia and Lithuania. At first the Jews were forced into waiting wagons, which took them to the trains. Even up to the last moments, some of the Nazis were not above taking money and goods from the frightened Jews who remained. The final liquidation of the Vilna ghetto began on September 23, 1943, and the entire grim business was over by December 28. In this even the police and administrators were not exempt. Balberyszski writes that there were ghetto police on board the train that took him and his son to Klooga, Estonia. On the trains and in the camps, people remembered the deeds of the policemen.[2]

41

people who did not belong to any partisan organizations. Some of them came with us. The majority did not.

Shulamit* and I were supposed to go to a building called the Spokaynis Engineering Workshop (Inzshini'eres Spokaynis Varshatn). We were supposed to go down to the cellar of the house and from there we would enter the city pipes. When we descended into the cellar, we had to reach an opening that led to the municipal sewer system. Abba Kovner stood by this hole with a **revolver in his hand**. He did not allow anyone who was not a member of the organization to enter. I really didn't know if he knew all the members of the organization or not. One young man with broad shoulders and a thick face was standing near the opening. I did not know who he was. I could read on his face that he was not being allowed to go into the sewers. I don't know where I got the courage, but I yelled out for him to go down into the hole. He entered in an instant. Until this day I don't know how he was able to get out of **the sewers** even though his shoulders were wider than the opening on Ignatovska Street.

REVOLVER IN HIS HAND

With the Nazis at the gates poised to liquidate the ghetto, partisans would only take those they knew – other members of the FPO – through the sewers. This meant that everyone else was left to fend for themselves. Many Jews were sent north and ended their lives in places like Klooga, where nightmarish atrocities occurred, which were so horrible that Red Army soldiers cried as they uncovered the half-burned corpses beneath human pyres. The victims were forced to construct the pyres themselves before they were shot. All this is not to say the FPO was wrong. They feared that the Russian led partisans in the forest would not take the old, weak, or sick, or those who came without arms or with children. With or without weapons, Jews were not safe outside the ghetto either and were often murdered.

Holding to this rule of only taking FPO members had terrible consequences. Abba Kovner turned his mother away. Rich Cohen writes that when Abba told her she could not come with them, she asked him, "What will become of me?" Kovner was haunted by this action for the rest of his life.[3]

THE SEWERS

Joseph Harmatz recounts: "We left Vilna on September 23, 1943, on the last day before the liquidation of the ghetto. We were told to gather at a workshop located at number 11 Rudnicki Street. The orders were clear – only members of the underground were allowed to enter. The escape had to be kept secret from family members, too. When I left, I left my younger brother Efraim and my mother behind. Later I found out that he was also a member of the underground, who, like me, was keeping the secret from his family.

"We escaped through the sewers. I was one of the last ones to descend, along with Rushka Korzak and Abba Kovner behind me. These were the sewers of the old city, and they were particularly narrow. The pipes were just wider than the width of our bodies, so we were forced to crawl on our knees, and at times on our stomachs. It was a very rainy day, and the stench inside the sewers was unbearable. Those in front would occasionally faint and block the path, probably due to the strong smells rising from the water. The people ahead of them got around this problem by dragging the unconscious people out to a juncture…. Eventually we reached an opening leading to the cellar of a church on Ignatovska Street, where two members of the Polish communist underground pulled us out.

"We were told to walk in pairs – it was night and it was still raining. The idea was to follow the pair ahead of us from a distance, but keep them in sight. We knew that we were supposed to leave the city, but in the event that we got lost we were told to go immediately to Keilis – a building outside the ghetto that housed a fur factory staffed with Jewish workers…."[4]

* The FPO member with whom Abrashe was paired.

When we **exited the canal** it was dark. We rested in a building. We were tired and wet. All the people were again divided in small groups, mostly a man with a woman. My companion at the time was Shulamit. She now lives in Israel. We walked hand in hand and were told to speak Polish. The key decision took place at the crossing that led to **Biala Vaka.**

We started walking and lost our way. The directive said that we should meet by the crossing, on the route that leads toward the forest. I asked Shulamit if she knew where the crossing was located. She answered in the affirmative. We arrived at a crossing but it led to Minsk and not Biala Vaka. We were going in the wrong direction. Then we started walking towards Biala Vaka. We were not far from the main highway. After about an hour of walking, we saw that the sun was coming up and decided to remain where we were for the day because travel was perilous. In the field, we found a deep hole where farmers dug for sand and crawled into it. I was carrying a box with eight grenades. I buried it in the sand. I dug out the sand with my hands and removed the immediate danger the grenades posed. I kept the bullets and revolver in my pockets.

When it became dark, we went toward the field. Then we saw farmers coming from the direction of Vilna on their way to Biala Vaka. We reached the road and walked along with the groups of farmers. Shulamit and I were close to one group. I started a conversation with one of the farmers. We had to cross a small bridge and saw that a lone German soldier was guarding it. This was a critical moment. We were saved from a terrible disaster because I was speaking to the farmer and because we were walking with the gentiles. We crossed the bridge without incident. When we reached the other side we felt that we had been saved from danger. We walked a kilometer and then veered to a side road that would lead us in the direction of the forest. At this point I

EXITED THE CANAL
Exiting the sewers proved risky. Some FPO members, led at this time by Shmuel Kaplinski, emerged from a sewer "practically in the back yard of the Central Police Station." They had entered the sewers at 4:00 PM, and it was now 7:00 PM. According to Isaac Kowalski, who participated in the escape, the FPO people went into two nearby stores to wait for their guides to arrive. Vitka Kempner came to the store where he was waiting and directed him to go to the Keilis work camp just outside Vilna, which he did.[5] [See note on Keilis in "A New Captain," chapter 8.]

The group that had been ahead of Joseph Harmatz was captured and killed.[6]

Based on Abrashe's memoir, it appears that he left in the group that included Joseph Harmatz, but that by some twist of fate, Abrashe and his companion made it out of Vilna proper and into the surrounding area without being captured. Judging by the extant accounts, they were the only twosome that managed to do so.

BIALA VAKA was a small town to the southwest of Vilna. It had been used as a work camp by the Nazis and was liquidated around the same time as Bezdani. The village lies between Vilna and the Rudnicki forest. Heading toward Minsk would have sent Abrashe and Shulamit to the southeast and far off course.[7]

was able to orient myself, more or less, about the direction we should take. In the distance we saw tall trees.

We encountered an old farmer. I greeted him with a hearty "good evening." He was a smart and good man. If I were an observant and believing Jew, I would have thought that we had met Elijah the prophet. The gentile asked us if we had escaped from the Germans. He knew that all Jews were being taken out of Vilna that day. I responded to his question and said, "Indeed we fled from Vilna to save ourselves. Please tell me how far the Rudnicki Forest is?"

He told me, "Go straight ahead and you will come upon a village. Do not enter the village. When you reach the first house, tap on the window. A man will come out of the house. You will ask him if he is Yasha. If he responds that he is Yasha Yarashevits, then you may ask him for directions to the forest. Please believe what I am telling you." This was the exact manner in which the old gentile spoke to me. I had a feeling that he was to be trusted.

I did what he told me to do. I banged on the window. It was nine in the evening and it was dark. A man came out and his name was Yasha Yarashevits. I asked him, "How close is the Rudnicki Forest?"

He answered that it wasn't far from here. "The forest begins to appear a few kilometers from here and it will lead you into the Rudnicki Forest." Then he inquired if we were hungry. I said that we were. He brought us a pitcher of milk and half a loaf of bread that he had baked in his house. We were so hungry. We hadn't had a drop of water in our mouths for two days. I looked at Shulamit's face and wondered if I looked as she did.

After Yasha gave us the milk and bread, he said that he would now direct us to the forest and give us instructions about where we should camp and where we should wait. "On many occasions Russian partisans pass by singing," he explained as he brought us to a thick part of the forest. This was not yet the Rudnicki Forest. He told us to rest there and listen to see if we heard the partisans coming. I thanked him with my whole heart and said my good-byes. We ate the bread and drank the milk. We did not sleep the entire night. We were hoping to meet the partisans. But no one came and we heard nothing. The sun was then beginning to shine. We looked around to get our bearings and saw mostly wooded areas. But in one direction I noticed an obviously larger forest with taller trees. We began walking toward it. After going several kilometers, we met a gentile who was gathering mushrooms. It was 7:00

AM. We were overcome with fear because of him. I greeted him in Russian. I asked him where the Rudnicki Forest was and how far it was from here. He responded that it was about ten kilometers from where we were. I pleaded with him to lead us there. He said that he had to go home immediately. I asked him: "Where do you live?"

"I live in the village of Vishintsi."

"How far is it from here?" He told us that it was about four kilometers away. "Are there any Germans around there?" I asked.

"Yes! In our village there are five Germans. They keep an eye over the farmers that chop wood for them to heat their quarters."

Then I took my gun from one pocket and placed it in my other pocket. Once he saw the revolver he understood me and said he would lead us to the Rudnicki Forest. He walked in front of me and led us for seven kilometers. Then he told us we had come to the beginning of the forest.

I oriented myself and saw that his directions were correct. I let him go, instructing him not to repeat what he saw. "We will meet again," I said. "I must find my battalion."

We went further into the forest. We hadn't heard from our friends from the ghetto and they hadn't heard from us. We were tired and laid down to rest. We still had the bread that Yasha gave us, which we ate with a great appetite. We decided to sleep over in this spot. We fell asleep and it rained. We were completely drenched. It was daybreak and the sun was beginning to come out, but we were not very happy. We were in a very dense forest, getting wetter and wetter. In the morning, the sun shone and we took off our outer garments so they could dry. All of a sudden I saw five men walking on the narrow forest road. We were sitting a few meters from the road and they noticed me. I did not know if they were partisans. One of them shot a bullet. We ran deeper into the forest and lay down as they were closing in on us. They were **speaking Russian** and I decided to greet them. One of the men asked me to identify myself. "I am from the Vilna ghetto. We are here to meet up with the partisans." Then he introduced himself, "I am Misha Laytenons. I am the commander for the Odessa Group of Moscow. Do you have a weapon?"

SPEAKING RUSSIAN

Joe Sabrin, Abrashe's son, explains that Abrashe spoke Russian, Polish, Yiddish, Hebrew, and later on learned English as well. The fact that these men spoke Russian in occupied Lithuania would have signaled to him that they were in fact partisans.

I answered, "Yes. I have a **revolver**."

I took it out and handed it over to him. He took my revolver and gave me his rations. My revolver was a nice Mauser that had been given to me in the Vilna ghetto. Then I asked him, "Where can I find the partisans?" He directed me to the place where his unit was located and told me that when we arrived there I should say that "Misha sent me here." We followed his instructions, and in an hour, we reached our destination. We met a group of thirty Russian partisans as well as a Jewish girl from Vilna. She was blond and resembled a Christian. Her name was Khvalye. Today she lives with her family in Montreal, Canada. She was given an assignment that required her to visit Vilna. The headquarters of the partisan brigade sent her there. We asked her if she knew of Khyene Borowska, Shmuel Kaplinski, and Abba Kovner, the people that accompanied us through the sewers. She told us, "They are a few kilometers from here, awaiting contact with a man named Anton. Anton is to lead them to the base where they will establish a partisan unit."

We ate and rested, and went out to search for them. We found them near Misha's group. Khyene called out to me. "Cadet," she said. This is a Polish expression used for someone who attended a military academy. When we were all together, she said that she knew nothing bad would happen to the cadet. They had a worse and more difficult trek than we had. German patrols shot at them. A partisan named Shurka Kevesh was wounded by the enemy. Khyene told us that they were waiting for the medic and that he did not come.

We decided to go further into the forest. We were tired, hungry, and thirsty. We passed through a plot of wet land, where the animals from villages situated in the area of the Rudnicki Forest would come to pasture during the day.

Desperately thirsty, people in our group started to drink the water in the muddy field. I told them that this was dangerous. "The water is full of bacteria. Only moisten your lips using a handkerchief or a kerchief." A lot of people listened to my warnings and others did not, but by good fortune nobody

REVOLVER

This episode was more dangerous than Abrashe lets on. A small group of armed Russian partisans encountering two Jews at the edge of the Rudnicki Forest a few days into a perilous journey across hostile territory could have behaved differently. Abrashe and Shulamit could easily have been murdered and robbed at this point. The fact that Misha takes Abrahse's revolver is telling because partisans do not relinquish their firearms. The penalty for losing a weapon in the forest is death. It was considerate of Misha to offer Abrashe food in exchange for his Mauser, but this was by no means a fair trade. It was more akin to robbery. Later on, Abrashe recounts how Misha returns his revolver after many months because of Abrashe's keen eye and ability to recognize a spy.[8] [See "The Nine-Year-Old Spy," chapter 9.]

became ill. We went on our way for about an hour and it started becoming dark. We stopped and rested among the thick trees but the ground was damp. We fell into a deep sleep. We were devoid of strength and the trip affected us physically. Before dawn, **Danke Loybatski** and I started searching for the place where the brigade staff was camped. We did this on our own. We did not ask anybody's permission. We understood that the staff headquarters was located close by. We walked about three kilometers and suddenly someone shouted, "*Stoy! Stoy!*" (Halt! Who are you?).

DANKE LOYBATSKI and his brother Imke [see note on the Loybatski brothers in "Partisan Heroes," chapter 8] were dedicated to the partisan cause. Imke went on to co-command the Third Unit with Abrashe after they arrived at the base. Both brothers were killed in combat while serving with the partisans.[9]

I responded, "I am FPO from Vilna." The sentry, Tevke Halpern, did not recognize me but he did recognize Danke. He had left for the forest earlier on with a small group of people. He ran to inform the staff that a group from Vilna had arrived. We ran back to inform the others that we had found the brigade staff headquarters. We went there and were well received. They shared their food with us. We were given a place where we could compose ourselves. It wasn't far from where we had previously been resting. We began our lives as partisans. Hundreds of mouths needed to be fed. Hundreds of people needed things, especially shoes. Ammunition was very low, but we started going on various missions. With each day our lives and the conditions improved steadily. To be a partisan was the only way to go. It was the only way that you had a chance of overcoming the murderous German machine. It was the only way of taking revenge against the Germans who spilled innocent Jewish blood. Work camps and concentration camps were a certain death sentence.

Chapter 7

A whole family was massacred in a flat at 10 Arëgalos Street. [The]seriously wounded head of this family, Akiva Pukhert, [a] metal craftsman in [the] Kovno factory "Drobe," managed to write, before his death, in his own blood on a wall, "Revenge!" his body was found next to this inscription.

Dimitri Ghelpernus[1]

The Forest

There were different partisan groups present in the forest, parachutists from the Soviet Union and many **Russians** who had escaped from German captivity. There were also Jews among them. The officers' staff started organizing the Lithuanian Brigade. There were a few Lithuanians in the brigade, too, but most of their countrymen were busier assisting the Germans than joining the partisans. There were 200 people from Kovno, ninety percent of them Jews. Their commander was **Kostia Radionov**, a Lithuanian who was not friendly to the Jews. Afterwards a small group of people arrived from Vilna. Together we totaled 350 people, men and women.

We began a new life as partisans. But the first few weeks in the forest were not very good ones. Khyene Borowska, Shmuel Kaplinski, and Abba Kovner, the leaders of the partisans, did not know how to begin the operation. At this time Russian partisans as

RUSSIANS

Groups of Russian soldiers had been living in the forests outside Vilna since the German invasion. When the Nazis overran the Soviets, these soldiers were trapped behind the lines, and knowing the Germans would show them no quarter, they hid in the forests. The first attempt by the Soviet Union to mount a guerrilla war failed because they used non-locals behind enemy lines. The guerrilla effort then began in earnest when six Lithuanian communists were parachuted into the Rudnicki forest in the second half of 1942. The FPO made initial contact with this group of Lithuanians, known as Alksnis, through a Jewish worker in the Biala Vaka labor camp. After this connection with the forest partisans was established and the FPO was recognized by the Soviets, the pressure mounted to escape and join the fight in the forest. But the FPO was devoted to fighting inside the ghetto and preserving Jewish life there. In the end, when it became obvious that the ghetto was being liquidated and that most of the ghetto inhabitants did not want to fight, the only option was the forest.[2]

KOSTIA RADIONOV is described by Arad as a commander in the Rudnicki Forest. He met with the Kovno Jews and behaved in a rude and arrogant manner.[3]

49

well as small groups of Jewish partisans were already operating under **Yurgis** in the Rudnicki forest. Yurgis was parachuted from Moscow. His real name was Zimanas and he had been a teacher of gifted students. He was assigned as first commissar of the so-called Lithuanian Partisan Brigade. Other Jews were also scattered among the Russian partisans.

Khyene Borowska wanted to retain a partisan ethos similar to that of the Jewish partisans who accompanied her into the forest. With the approval of Yurgis, she was appointed commissar. A sizeable proportion of the partisans belonged to various Zionist organizations. I was appointed vice-commander to her husband, Kaplinski. My appointment was for her purposes. She knew I would be able to replace her husband on many missions.

In the forest, the Jewish leaders introduced an atmosphere of fear. They surrounded themselves with members of the Komsomol (Communist Youth Party) and with devoted, practicing communists, who would provide information about other people's conversations. Everyone was afraid to speak because of these informers.

The leadership of the Jewish partisans also decided early on to send away a group of 110 men and women to another forest situated 120 kilometers from Rudnicki. I was assigned to go along with the group they sent away. A half hour before the plan was to become a reality, Khyene ordered me to remain in the Rudnicki Forest. Everybody feared her because of her communist manner and she leveraged this fear against the fighters.

The 110 fighters were sent away with an insignificant amount of arms. They went to the White Russian forests and met up with **Markov,** who was a regiment leader. He was a teacher by profession, from the city of Swienciany, and a member of the Communist Party. The name of the forest where the group was being sent was Nacza. The roads to it were very dangerous because they passed through many villages and open fields,

YURGIS was one of the first Lithuanian partisans to be parachuted behind the lines by the Soviets as they began a campaign of guerilla warfare against the Nazis. "His real name was Henech [Henri] Ziman [Zimanas], and he was a Jew. He did not reveal this in the forest and passed for a real Lithuanian.… Before the war, he had been a Lithuanian language teacher in the Shalom Aleichem Gymnasium in Kovno. In 1940-41, he was editor-in-chief of the communist daily in Kovno, *Tiessa* (Truth). He retreated with the Red Army, and in the middle of 1943 he parachuted from a Soviet plane into White Russia."[4]

MARKOV arrived in the Narocz Forest in 1942 and expanded his unit to include over 300 men. Markov was the commander who accepted the Vilna Jews in Narocz prior to the FPO's escape through the sewers. He also gave the order to disarm the Jewish unit known as "Vengeance."[5]

and bands of **"White Poles"** roamed the area. They were real bandits. They were worse than the real Nazis. Their motto was "kill the Communists, kill the Jews." It was criminal sending the group to their deaths. I was certain that the Rudnicki Forest was large enough to accommodate them as well as thousands of other Jews. But the leadership of the Jewish partisans was afraid of the reaction of the non-Jews in the area.

After the group left for the **Nacza Forest**, our group moved to another area in the Rudnicki Forest. There it was decided to build dugouts (**bunkers**) and establish a permanent base. We were divided into two units. The first one was called Nekamah Nemer (vengeance takers), and it was led by Abba Kovner. The name of the second unit was Far'n Nitzahon (For Victory), which was headed by Shmuel Kaplinski. I was his deputy.

Each unit consisted of 120 individuals, about 85 men and 35 women. The commissar for both units was Khyene Borowska. She had the last word over all matters, and gave instructions to both Kovner and Kaplinski.

After building the dugouts, our next objective was to **obtain food**. This was a serious undertaking. We had insignificant amounts of arms, and the weapons we did have were in the hands of men and women of the Vilna ghetto who had never fired a shot. Forty men, including myself, were assigned for these missions. Since we didn't have any experience in these matters, we were assigned a commander from

"WHITE POLES" (THE POLISH FOLK ARMY)

As the war progressed, large groups of the Polish "Home Army" began to appear in the forests around Vilna. Their goal was to fight the Russians and establish themselves on their own land as the Nazi menace retreated. Many of these Poles viewed the Jews as communist collaborators who participated in the destruction of Poland, and sought to eradicate the Jews along with the communists. Yitzhak Arad was among the partisans serving under Markov and was already in the forests prior to the arrival of the FPO. In his memoir, he recalls that fighting the White Poles was often more difficult than engagements against the Nazis, since they were predictable and operated on the main roads. The White Poles, however, fought and moved in the same ways as the partisans themselves, but were often vastly superior in number. The partisans called them White Poles to distinguish them from the Poles who were pro-Soviet.[6]

THE NACZA FOREST

Arad writes that in November 1943, the brigade command sought to establish partisan operations in southern Lithuania in an area known as the Nacza Forest. Yurgis sent over one hundred Jewish fighters with "eleven rifles and two sub-machine guns" under the command of Berl Szeresznyevski. The mission was a failure, as the forest was entirely inhabited by White Poles, and the partisans themselves were under-armed, under-trained, and under-fed.[7]

BUNKERS (ZEMLANKAS)

These were the forest huts the partisans dwelled in. They were dug into the ground and framed with a timber roof that was then overlain with layers of brushwood, dirt, and clay. Although they were often stuffy, these Zemlankas provided the partisans with shelter that was well insulated against the cold.[8]

OBTAIN FOOD

Abrashe is describing what the partisans called an "economic action." This was the euphemism for the armed searches and appropriation of food, which they were forced to conduct in the nearby villages. As Abrashe explains, the point was to take food from more distant villages and farmhouses, as it was wise to remain on a friendly footing with the closest villagers who, if angered, could become a security threat. The partisans obtained most of their food and clothing through these "economic actions."[9] [See note on supplies in "Death to Fascists," chapter 8.]

the Russian group, whose name was **Alyeko**. They had been in the forest for a longer time than we had. The commander assigned to us was Vanke Laytenent. I was jealous of him since he possessed an automatic weapon and I only had a gun. Of the forty fighters who went on this – their first – mission, one-third were armed and the rest carried sticks.

CAPTAIN ALYEKO was among the first partisans parachuted into the Rudnicki Forest together with a small group under his command.[10]

We arrived at a village in the darkness of night. It was located 20 kilometers from the forest. I do not remember the name of the village. The forty of us were divided into units of three and four people who set out to obtain food from the farmers. Every farmer was required to harness his horse to his wagon. When the food was gathered it would be loaded on a wagon. They would load potatoes, flour, salt, grits, clothing, and pigs. The pigs would be killed before loading them on the wagon.

The First Fatality

The partisan Shmuel Shapira was a butcher by trade, so he had been sent to procure meat for us. Just when he was in a stall killing a pig, he heard a shot. It had come from the farmer's house. The farmer, whose pig was being taken away, was not very happy about what we were doing. Vanke Laytenent, the Russian assigned as our commander for the mission, was stationed not far away from the house. He took out his automatic and shot back at the farmer at the very moment that Shmuel Shapira left the stall. In the darkness of the night, Vanke, not knowing that it was Shapira and thinking it was the farmer, shot three bullets at him. All of them hit Shapira. He was mortally wounded. They placed him in my wagon.

NO POSSIBILITY OF PERFORMING AN OPERATION

Leon Berk was a doctor assigned to the Sovyetskaya Beloruss partisan unit not far from the Rudnicki Forest. Aside from the atrocities he witnessed his fellow partisans commit, Berk's major complaint was the lack of medical provisions and equipment. Rusty saws were sometimes used to amputate limbs. Isaac Kowalski recalls participating in an amputation where he was the doctor's "helper." No anesthetic was available when they removed a partisan's leg. Kowalski buried the leg outside the hut when they were finished.[11]

The provisioning operation was speeded up. I had the wounded partisan with me and was the first to leave. We returned to the forest. The mortally wounded partisan fought death for two days. The three bullets remained in his lungs. There was **no possibility of performing an operation**. On the third day, he died. He was the first Jewish casualty among the fighters of the Rudnicki Forest. His memory should be everlasting!

To get back to the forest with the wounded partisan, I

took the shortest route. We had to cross a bridge that was guarded by a German. Three to four hundred meters before the bridge, there were Germans on watch, but at that moment, they were sleeping. I wanted to arrive at the base as quickly as possible with the mortally wounded Shapiro. I wanted him to get help from Dr. Finkelstein. Commander Vanke was caught off guard by the route I took and the chance I was taking. I was now a half a kilometer from the bridge. As we approached it, the road curved away from it. When we were a quarter of a kilometer from the bridge, I called out that everybody should ready their guns. We arrived at the bridge. The Germans' watch was coming to an end. I drove the wagon at top speed. The lone German guard was so surprised to see a partisan passing by that he became frozen with fright. He couldn't believe what had just happened. He did not dare shoot at us as we crossed to the other side.

We continued another half a kilometer into the forest when Vanke the Russian ordered us to stop our wagons. He asked me how I dared travel this route. "Who gave you the right to drive in this direction?" I answered him that we were carrying wounded partisans. He laughed. I did not feel anger in his tone and I was sure he would inform the general staff, especially Yurgis, about what I had done. We finally arrived at the base and carried the severely wounded Shapiro into the hut. The doctor concluded that he had been shot three times and the bullets were in his lungs. The prognosis was not a good one. Two days passed and there was no improvement in his condition. On the third day, he died. When we took other missions that brought us near the bridge, the Germans stationed there did not shoot at us. They just wanted to sit in peace and not be sent to the Russian front.

The First Mine of the Rudnicki Forest

A few weeks later, when I was still in the Second Unit and representing Kaplinski, I was appointed to a group led by Abba Kovner, the commander of the First Unit. Our mission was to blow up a train traveling on the Kovno-Vilna line. It was going from Konigsberg to the front. Aside from Kovner and myself, the other partisans assigned to the group were Abrashe Tshuzshy, Rashl Markovitsh, a smart and courageous young lady, and **Rushka Korzak**, another

RUSHKA KORZAK was a leading figure in Hashomer Hatza'ir in Vilna under the Soviet occupation, when the movement was forced to go underground. She escaped with the FPO through the sewers, carrying the group's archives and Kovner's poetry. She was the first FPO fighter to reach Palestine. Upon arriving, she was forced into a British camp where she was made to strip for delousing, a term which the Nazis used when sending Jews to the gas chambers. She was among the first to testify to the Palestinian Jewish community about what the Jews had undergone in Vilna.[12]

courageous young woman. We left late, after lunch. We had to walk a distance of 20 kilometers. We knew our directions. The mines weighed almost fourteen kilograms. Each of us carried them at one time or another during the march. We reached a village that was near the train tracks. At the outskirts of this village, we called out to a peasant. We told him that we needed his help. We wanted him to lead us to an approach to the railroad tracks that was not mined, since we knew that the Germans would heavily mine all of them. We also needed to know where the tracks went over a rise or high place so that when the bombs went off more cars would roll down and be destroyed.

The peasant had no choice but to fulfill our orders. He took us to a place that met our specifications. Kovner and I climbed up to the tracks and placed the mines. The other three remained behind watching the peasant, and in case we were attacked, they would protect us by opening fire against the enemy. I laid the mines underneath the tracks and Kovner installed the fuse that would ignite the bombs. A 50-meter-long cord extended from the fuse. While Kovner was holding the fuse, his hands and feet began to shake. I saw that he was in a dangerous position and that the fuse could explode in his hand. I then spoke some strong words to him in Russian. They weren't very nice words, but they allowed him to regain his composure and he calmly inserted the fuse into the bomb. We climbed down from the tracks and Kovner grabbed the cord. The train was now a few meters from the mines. Kovner pulled the cord and there was a frightening explosion of yellow fire. The train received what it deserved. The tanks it was transporting turned upside down. They made a ringing sound.*

We all escaped into the nearby forest. The Germans began shooting light rockets. We laughed at them and went back into the forest. A few days later our spies went to assess the damage caused by the mines. They reported that the Vilna to Kovno line was shut down for two whole days – forty-eight hours. Many Nazis had been killed and wounded. A great many tanks and artillery pieces had fallen out of the railway cars. It was a successful operation. In the future, we carried out this type of operation as often as possible. Unfortunately,

---

* Isaac Kowalski, *A Secret Press in Nazi Europe* (New York: Shengold Publishers, Inc., 1969), p. 269, tells the same story. The only difference between his and Abrashe's accounts is that Kowalski recalls that Szabrinski pulled the detonator cord, whereas Abrashe states it was Abba Kovner who pulled the cord. Both Szabrinski and Kowalski report that the cars made a ringing sound.

some of the partisans fell in action, but we forced the Nazis to travel by night. Each unit endeavored to perform such operations. The German war machine began to understand the partisan's courage and power.

The Second Mine

About a month after planting the first device, we were given another assignment to detonate explosives. Shmuel Kaplinski was the commander and I was his deputy. A short time later, he would be removed from this position and I would be appointed in place of him. In the meantime, he was the commander and I obeyed his orders. I remember that five partisans went on the mission. One participant was Yitzhak Tshuzshy, but I don't recall the names of the others. We set out in the same direction as we had for our first mine laying operation, the railroad track that went from Kovno to Vilna and from there, to the Russian front.

When we reached the first village, which was ten kilometers from the forest, we noticed a wagon parked next to one of the houses with no one in it. I looked in the wagon and saw a mine. It looked exactly like the ones we were carrying. Then we looked through the window of the lighted house and saw a group of four Russian partisans. They were drinking. Our group quickly walked away. I did not want to meet them. It is not that I was afraid of them, but I didn't want to have to walk with drunkards – this was an important mission. We moved quickly to distance ourselves from the Russians. We came to the train tracks, but not to the same place as on the first operation. We used a side road to enter the village. The gentile we awakened was friendlier than the one on the first assignment. We went to the tracks with him. The location he took us to was not as good as the first spot. The tracks weren't as elevated as the first time, but it would do. I waited for about half an hour for the train to arrive in order to destroy it. We heard it coming and Yitzhak and I, with speed and nimbleness, planted the mine. We had to be very careful. One mistake and you could destroy both your hands.

I was carrying the string and we ran about 50 meters away from the rails. There we lay down for a few minutes. The train then traveled over the mine. I pulled the string and there was a great explosion. The train was destroyed. From where we were, we could hear the cries of wounded men. They started shooting their guns and launching rockets into the dark sky. The shooting had no effect on us. We partisans with the good gentile moved further away from the scene. We arrived at the base, tired and happy. Shmuel Kaplinski was very happy. Khyene Borowska, the political commissar and Shmuel's future wife, complimented me (the cadet) on my good work. (She always called me "the cadet.") A few days later I met Meir Grozni, the commander of a special partisan unit. I told him that I had seen him drinking whiskey in the village the other night, but I didn't want to disturb him so I left him alone. He told me that I had outcompeted him.

The Third Mine

The German trains stopped traveling at night because of the partisan's actions. So now they were traveling by day under the watch of the German and Ukrainian guards. In our unit we had a former Red Army soldier by the name of Boris. He was a young man, about twenty-three years of age. He had been captured in Leningrad, so we called him the Leningrader. Boris was an expert at fighting for the partisan cause. He told me that he could lay a mine by night and ignite it by day as the train passed over the explosives. I asked how he could make a fuse when we didn't have automatic fuses. I told him that it was not our practice to blow up trains by day. He answered that "In Leningrad we also did not have automatic fuses, but we blew up the trains by day anyhow."

He explained to me that in our case, we typically detonate our mines using a short metal wire with a bent ear that holds up the spring, which in turn holds up the hammer that detonates the fuse. A long string is tied to this. When the time comes to detonate the mine, we pull the string and that, in turn, pulls out the wire that holds up the spring, and the hammer causes the explosion. This cannot be done if trains travel by day because you need the cover of darkness to conceal yourself.

Now he described how, rather than using a metal wire, we could use lead from a pencil. This was dangerous work, of course. The fuse can explode in your hand. The diameter of the fuse was one centimeter; therefore, the lead had to be able to withstand the pressure of the spring. There was another danger. When you installed the fuse in the mine, it had to be placed where the two rails are fastened together. When the train crosses a point on the rail, the rail bends a little. This is a fact. So when the rails bend, they put the squeeze on the fuse. The lead is broken and detonation occurs.

I understood what he was telling me very well and I agreed with him. I also knew it was very dangerous. The danger came when the mine was buried, since the place where the lead was positioned in the fuse was so narrow, there was a real possibility for an explosion to occur. Boris responded that he would take on this job. We chose a train to blow up, the Lida to Vilna train, and the spot for the explosion. It was about one kilometer from the Rudnicki Fortress. They called the place a "fortress" because a bridge built of thick steel was located there. It crossed the Vilayke River and it was guarded by about twenty Germans and Lithuanians. When the trains traveled by night, they would often go out on patrol. But when the trains stopped traveling at night, the patrols also stopped. We discovered this information and found it to be accurate. This is why I decided the bridge was the right place to plant a mine, employing Boris's method of constructing them. I assigned three partisans for the job. The first one was Boris. The second one was Abrashe Tshuzshy, the *shohet*, a heroic young man. The third was Lyanye (Leon) Tshibuk. He was a Pole who joined our forces. His father and brother were members of the Polish Folk Army who were unabashed anti-Semites. Lyanye was the exception. He was a trustworthy soldier. They went to plant the mines, at a distance of 15 kilometers. Boris planted the mines. The others were hiding in the bushes about 100 meters from the spot. Due to security reasons, they all waited for the explosion. At 8:00 AM, a train was coming from Lida. Then there was an awesome explosion. They ran away. A day later we discovered that it was a civilian train. The passengers included Poles, Lithuanians, and Germans. About seventy people were wounded and about twenty were killed. This was a successful operation. The other units also began to carry out such missions. Boris became very popular. The Germans increased their patrols along the train tracks, which did not stop the partisans from continuing their operations and dispensing retribution to the bloody enemy. This is how it was.

Chapter 8

*"Motl Gopstein, a young man from the Third Unit, received a bullet
in the stomach. He knew he was going to die. He yelled to his
friends: 'Escape and I will cover you.' He did not want to be captured
by the Germans, so he took out his gun and killed himself."*

Abrashe Szabrinski

Death to Fascists

After three weeks, the group of 110 fighters who had been sent to the Nacza Forest returned to our base. One of their men – his name was Moyshe – was standing watch and a White Pole shot him. The fighters came back in small groups. They were weak and sick, and their feet were raw and sore. When they entered our base, Khyene Borowska, Abba Kovner, and Shmuel Kaplinski made it known that they were **not welcome**. They were not accepted in either of the two units and were kept one kilometer away from them. They ate what Khyene, Kovner, and Kaplinski gave them. They remained in this situation for several weeks. A few of the sick were accepted into the two groups and Dr. Garfinkel attended them.

Henri Zimanas, who was called Yurgis, received orders from Moscow telling him to travel deep into Lithuania to recruit Lithuanians into the partisan units. A member of the brigade staff replaced him. His name was Mitseika, but he was known as **Gavris.**

NOT WELCOME

The Jewish partisan commanders had to deal with the fact that their Russian hosts did not want to accept more Jewish refugees into their midst. The decision to turn away Jews was made not only on anti-Semitic grounds; it also reflected the reality that the Russian partisans considered themselves "fighting men" and did not think it advisable to add unarmed men, women, and children to their ranks. This argument may appear logical, yet there were some very successful family camps that proved otherwise, the most famous being Beilski's camp. A partisan camp that included many noncombatants was not necessarily a liability. Such a camp was capable not only of pooling resources, but also knowledge of various trades. As Abrashe describes, one of his partisans had to be forcibly pulled from active duty because he was a shoemaker, and their unit needed shoes more than they needed fighters at that time.[1] [See "The Shoemaker," chapter 9.]

Of **GAVRIS**, Arad writes, "Marians Mitseika, whose nom de guerre was Gavris, came to the Rudniki forests from the Narocz forests in September 1943 to prepare a base for relocating the southern headquarters of the Soviet-Lithuanian partisans under the command of Zimanas.[2]

He was a member of the Communist Party. He had a Jewish wife who disappeared, though no one knows what happened. We were good friends. Others informed me that he liked me very much. He viewed me as a military man.

I visited him in his home and spoke to him about the 109 people who had come back from the Nacza Forest. I asked him why there was no place for them to settle. My words impressed him. He visited the two units. He ordered Khyene to place the 109 people with the first two units. She had to obey his orders. The group was then divided into two units of its own. A place was established for them two kilometers from us. They became the Third and Fourth Units. One unit [the Fourth] was called *Kamf* (ordeal) and its commander was Imke Loybatski. He was a member of the Young Communist League. I later discovered that he was Khyene's choice. The Third Unit was called Death to Fascists. Bodrisn and I were assigned to be their commanders.

GATHER FOOD

Joseph Harmatz recalls that during his time in the forest, "Two very different challenges faced us: one was to attack the Germans wherever they were: in their bases, stationed at specific posts, en route from one location to another. The second, and by far the most dangerous, was to provide an ongoing supply of sustenance for our people. This meant regular expeditions to the local villages to obtain food, a dangerous mission and one we faced throughout our entire period in the forests, and as time wore on, it became more and more of a problem.... We suffered more casualties from our food-gathering expeditions than we did blowing up trains, bridges, railway lines, and telegraph poles in our fight against the Germans."[3]

I knew that the responsibility would fall on my shoulders and I accepted it with joy. As soon as the two units settled in the new place, under the open sky, Gobris came and read the orders of the day. When he finished and they were standing in two rows, I appealed to them. I said, "If you want to become partisans, then you must follow your commanders. We must take a trip to a rich village and **gather food**. I know that some of you are weak; therefore I ask only for volunteers." Thirteen people volunteered for the food gathering expedition. Our mission was a complete success. We brought back fourteen boxes of all kinds of food. I became very experienced in these kinds of operations. By this point, I had scouted the area many times and oriented myself to it.

The two units were able to refresh themselves in a few days. We started building dugouts (underground bunkers). I appointed Nahum Koganovitsh, the head of the detail, to build them. He was a capable person and a good partisan, who was able to lead and achieve quick results. Within a few weeks, we were settled in. We were no worse than the other two detachments.

Aside from the construction of these dwellings, other things contributed to the feeling that a certain degree of normalcy was taking hold in the camps. We were beginning to receive arms. The forest had one radio contact with Moscow. When the airplanes flew over to bomb the enemy, or to parachute **supplies** or soldiers,* it was our task to signal them and guide them to their targets. We had a system in place where we would signal our position by burning letters into the ground. A letter *M* meant Moscow. A flyer from Moscow would recognize the letter *M* and unload his cargo at

SUPPLIES

Isaac Kowalski described how, "Often I would be in a group that knew in advance about the scheduled arrival of a plane because we would be assigned to the unit that had to carry wood to a large clearing to prepare it for the parachute drop later in the evening. After dark we would make a large bonfire to guide the pilots. The sacks would be dropped when the brigadier signaled with a colored flare."[4]

the place where the letter was burning. We received various types of equipment including automatic weaponry, regular guns with bullets, demolition ordinance, and explosives to destroy military trains. We also received medicine and cigarettes.

Khyene considered herself the lord of the forest and boss of the Jewish partisans. Her attitude did not bother me. What did disturb me was the way she ingratiated herself with the Christian, Russian, and Lithuanian commanders. After spending a few weeks with my unit, she called me in for a meeting to talk about where we would be foraging for food. She ordered me not to go into the areas where units 1 and 2 searched for provisions. Instead I had to travel in the other direction. But the area to which she was sending me was more dangerous because it crossed the train tracks the Nazis used, and well-armed Germans and Lithuanians were stationed there. I had no choice. She was the commissar. I did not want to complain to the brigade commissar, so I set off in the new direction. The first attempt was fine. On the second try, we were shot at. We barely escaped with our lives.

A thought entered my mind after the second expedition. Near the edge of the forest there was a village from which we were not permitted to take food. The reason for this policy was that the villagers assisted the spies of our brigade. They were given special privileges and we weren't allowed to take anything from them.

---

* Moscow delivered important items to the partisans by airdrop, typically on their return flights from bombing the Nazis farther west. See Kowalski, *A Secret Press in Nazi Europe*, pp. 242–43.

I took a few animals and some potatoes and other supplies from them. We did not take a lot of food. I knew that in the morning the brigade staff would interrogate me. And so it was. In the morning, they called me in. "What was the meaning of this? What right do you have to take food from them?" In response to their questioning, I told them the truth. "Commissar Borowska told me to go in that new direction to gather food, and a few times I was shot at." They ordered me to return the animals and allowed me to take the direction of my choice. Khyene was very angry at the decision, but she couldn't do anything about it.

Reconnaissance

When I was appointed to be the commander of the Third Unit, Shloymele was also assigned to that unit. When we went on missions, Shloymele would follow me. He was a good partisan. He was especially good with the horses and wagons. One time we went on a food gathering expedition. I didn't go to the village but to areas where the farmers had their own parcels of land. These were called **khutors**. I divided my unit into groups of three partisans each. The most responsible of the three was assigned to serve as group commander. They all knew their responsibilities. I chose Shloymele as one of the commanders. Another partisan and I remained at the point where the others would return with the food and then go back to the base, 25 kilometers away. The clock was ticking, but Shloymele and his group had not yet returned to our meeting place. He was one and a half kilometers away. I decided to go there with another partisan and find out what was happening. We went to the house where Shloymele was supposed to be. When we got there, I became ashen. Shloymele was dead drunk and had not loaded any food on the wagon. I wanted to shoot him on the spot.

KHUTORS were single tenant land holdings in Eastern Europe. After the war, these farms were wiped out by the Soviet system of collectivization.[5]

In order to calm down, I gave him two stinging slaps across the face and took away his gun. He started coming to himself. I told the farmer to bring all the food he had hidden and we would divide it evenly. He knew he was in danger of being shot so he brought out all the hidden items and food from beneath the hay. I removed everything that he had and we loaded two wagons of goods from the farmer.

When we arrived at the base, we wanted to put Shloymele on trial. He never again became inebriated. Fortune smiled upon him. He could very easily have lost his life because of his lack of sobriety. Today he lives in Israel. I believe he remembers all these experiences very well.

In the Third Unit, we still had to build dugouts. In the evening we sat by the fire and warmed ourselves. While sitting around the fire one night, I found myself looking into the eyes of a young man who had a light colored beard. He hadn't shaved in a while, and his eyes were telling a story. I asked him for his name. He said that it was Belkyevitsh. "Why aren't you shaven?" I asked him.

"I don't have a razor or soap."

In my jacket, I had a towel, soap, and a razor. I told him he should take a shave, wash, and return the items. When he came back shaven and washed he looked completely different. Then I asked him if he had served in the Polish army. He said yes, and that he had the rank of corporal. I put him in charge of a light machine gun.

A short while later we went on a mission to procure supplies. Khyene Borowska, Shmuel Kaplinski, and Abba Kovner assigned us the area in which we were supposed to operate, the one I mentioned earlier that was very dangerous. On that occasion, upon returning from the operation, Lithuanians attacked us. It was a battle from which we needed to retreat, and we needed to retreat from different positions. We were lucky that we didn't take any losses. Everybody returned to their meeting place. The last to come back was Belkyevitsh, with his machine gun on his shoulder. He was a good partisan and a really good fighter. I did not make a mistake in giving him the machine gun. We were all liberated at the same time and today he lives with his wife in Florida.

When Imke Loybatski and I were assigned as the commanders of the Third and Fourth Units, we instituted identical regulations pertaining to order and discipline, those which were in force in the other units. I named Monyek Rodzyevitsh as the head of a *razvedka*. Their task was to find rich villages and keep up good relations with the farmers there. They needed be able to distinguish between the farmers who could be trusted and those who were to be avoided. They were also responsible for finding out about the German army's movements.

RAZVEDKA

"It is impossible to precisely translate the Russian word *razvedka* into any foreign language. It is usually rendered as 'reconnaissance' or 'spying' or 'intelligence gathering.' A fuller explanation of the word is that it describes any means and any actions aimed at obtaining information about an enemy, analyzing it, and understanding it properly."[6]

The village of Papishki was situated west of the forest. Another village that also had the same name, Papishki, was located east of the forest in the direction of Vilna. The village of Rudnicki was seven kilometers to the west, and a German garrison of thirty well-armed soldiers was stationed there. The garrison also had two regular cannons in its arsenal that were able to reach a distance of 50 kilometers.

Monyek Rodzyevitsh traveled the roads almost exclusively by himself or with one or two other partisans. He would attempt to gather information from the local Christians. There was one Christian who lived in the village of Papishki that he trusted. He was a farmer with a wife and two sons. On December 19, 1943, there was a very big snowfall and we were able to ride in a sleigh. Monyek was getting ready to visit the Christian to receive fresh information, and he told me that he was going to take one horse and the sleigh that our camp possessed. He also told me he was going to bring along Moyshe Stritsyanskin and that they were going to Papishki. I advised him that he should go by foot. He pleaded with me to be allowed to use the horse and sleigh, persuading me that his visit to the Christian would be a quick one. I agreed.

On this particular day, the gentile's two sons had gone to a mill in the city to grind corn and flour. They had to pass through Rudnicki and would return in the evening. That same day some Germans came to the village and went to the farmer. It was late in the afternoon and had started becoming dark when Monyek and Moyshe arrived at the farmer's house. They encountered the Germans. They tried to escape. Monyek immediately received a bullet in his back but remained alive. They captured Moyshe and placed him on the sleigh that had transported them there. They tied Monyek up to the back of the sleigh with a rope. This was how the good partisan, Monyek Rodzyevitsh, was caught by the Germans and experienced an excruciating death. Moyshe was brought to the Vilna Gestapo. They interrogated him and he told them everything. They found out all the units' names. Where he was killed I do not know. We were very angry about Monyek's death. I went to Commissar Gobris and asked him if we should eliminate the farmer's family. He undertook an investigation since he was the brigade staff's head of reconnaissance. He determined that the farmer was innocent of collusion. In fact, it seemed that the Nazis had suspected him of assisting the partisans.

Chaim Lazar

Chaim Lazar was a partisan and a group commander with the Second Unit. He was a serious fighter you could rely on. Kaplinski sent him and a group of partisans to blow up a train loaded with Nazis and military hardware. They knew the train would pass by at 4:00 PM. Chaim took a beautiful girl by the name of Hayele Shapira with the group. After the war, he married her. The train was running late. It was already 5:00 PM and the train had not yet arrived at the designated spot. I am telling the story as the people who were there told it to me. When the time came to lay the mine, the fuse that was supposed to ignite the mine blew up in Chaim's hand. Three of his fingers were torn off, and the others just barely escaped with their lives. They returned to the forest. Vasye, a Russian doctor from one of the units, operated on Chaim. Little by little, he came around. After the war, in Moscow, they made him a hand protector. He was left with only one hand. I was in the Third Unit then, but a short while later, I returned to the Second Unit.

A New Captain

Imke and I had been the commanders for two months when two escapees from the **Ninth Fort** in Kovno arrived. The Nazis imprisoned thousands of people, including Jews, in this fortress, where they had set up work and living areas. It was also an execution site where Jews were being shot. One of the escapees was called **Vasilyenko**. His real name was Vaselnitski, and he was a Jew from Odessa with the

CHAIM LAZAR

Lazar wrote the following testimony about this incident:

"On one of the days of spring in the year 1944, a feeling of anticipation and excitement ran through the camp. The information was received that the Brigade Command had put at our disposal a quantity of explosives that would suffice to blow up four of the enemy's trains…for a number of nights, one after the other the political Commissar Diadlis (Didalyis) and the commanders of the units, Abba Kovner, and Shmuel Kaplinsky at the head of a unit of explosives experts, would go out and then return to the camp crowned with victory. We only have one explosive device left in our possession and the Command decided that I am worthy of the honor of detonating it…in the second shift we approach the tracks…. We already hear the clatter of the approaching train. I raise the trigger and bring it close to the charge to fix it into place. Suddenly a terrifying sound explodes in my ears and I feel a sharp pain in my right hand. It turns out that one of the fighters hiding in the thicket inadvertently pulled the cable and caused the bomb to explode prematurely. If it had happened even a tenth of a second later, the explosives would already have been inside the mine and the three of us would have been torn to shreds."[7]

THE NINTH FORT

"At the end of the nineteenth and beginning of the twentieth century a network of fortresses was set up around Kovno…. Surrounded by a barbed wire fence, they had high embankments and deep pits. Now the forts had become execution sites. The Ninth Fort became an execution block not only for residents of Kovno but for the citizens of a number of European countries."[8]

CAPTAIN VASILYENKO escaped from the Ninth Fort with a group of Jews and other European prisoners on Christmas day, 1943. Afterwards, the group wrote a report detailing the horrors that had taken place there. It described the atrocities the Nazis committed and the attempts to cover them up by exhuming and burning the bodies, and grinding the remnants to dust. Vasilyenko along with the rest of the group fled first to the Kovno ghetto, but left on January 6, 1943, seeking refuge in the Rudnicki Forest, where they were embraced by the partisans.[9]

rank of captain. The second was called Krokleys and he was a Lithuanian. Both were members of the Communist Party. They were assigned as commanders in place of Imke and me. Imke remained with his division, but I asked Bodrisn to be reassigned to the Second Unit. He complied with my wish. I again became Kaplinski's advisor. The members of the Second Unit were happy that I rejoined them. They knew they could rely on me. Kaplinski seldom went on missions and the same was true of Abba Kovner.

When fifty men and women came from **Keilis**, Khyene Borowska, Shmuel Kaplinski, and Abba Kovner were also not interested in saving these Jews, even though most of them were friends of the Vilna FPO. A few thousand Jews remained in the Keilis and HKP camps.

Around this time, I began to ask Khyene about **Sonya Madeysker**. "What is she doing in the city? Who is she working for there? The ghetto has been liquidated, but the Jews from Keilis haven't been brought over yet." She would avoid giving me a clear answer. I warned her that in the end Sonya would lose her life for no purpose, and indeed this is what happened.

When we were in the first settled area in the forest, the place from which we sent out the 110 people, three women and two children from the Vilna ghetto came to the forest. The secret patrols caught them two kilometers from our camp and informed us that they were being detained.

The refugees had arrived with the help of good Christians who had given them directions. The commanders did not allow them to enter the camp*. On that particular day, I was leading a special unit charged with bringing back food. Khyene also assigned Joseph Harmatz, a member of the communist youth organization, to accompany me. At that time there was a Vilna man known as Didalyis in the forest. He had been parachuted in from Moscow

KEILIS was a small work camp located on Wiwulska Street just outside the Vilna ghetto, which continued to operate because its "Jews produced fur coats for the freezing German troops on the front."[10]

SONYA MADEYSKER
She joined the FPO early on and was a devoted partisan who had run numerous missions both before and after the escape from the ghetto. She played an important role in helping Isaac Kowalski get the secret Jewish printing press up and running. She was also among those who informed Isaac Wittenberg that the FPO had decided unanimously that he should give himself up to the Gestapo. According to Yitzhak Arad, the FPO established contact with Sonya, still in Vilna, as soon as they were established in the forest. She died just prior to the city's liberation by the Soviet Army. When the Gestapo stormed her rooms, she shot herself but did not die until days later inside the Lukiski Prison.[11]

*Yurgis had given the order to turn away Jews. Yitzhak Arad writes that "When Zimanas [Yurgis] came to Rudnicki in October 1943, he took charge of all units belonging to the Soviet-Lithuanian partisan movement in southern Lithuania. One of his first orders was to put an end to unarmed groups coming into the forest from Vilnius. That was a hard blow for those who wanted to save Jews and enlarge the Jewish force in Rudnicki."[12]

along with a group. He wanted to be with Jews. He served as a commissar. In Lithuanian, Didalyis means "small." His real name was Isor Shmid and he presently lives in Israel. When I was ready to set out to procure food, he called me into Khyene's dugout. There they ordered me to take the three women and the two children to a village at least 20 kilometers away and leave them there. Didalyis warned me that I shouldn't have any mercy. I did not respond. I set out with my group on our food gathering operation, and knew what I was going to do about the situation. We went on our way without speaking to each other. We reached the area where the women and children were being detained. The partisans of the new watch were accompanying us.

I called the women and told them that I had orders to take them with us and arrange for accommodations in a village. Then one of them called out and said: "Sonny boy. We're not going anywhere. You may kill us right now in this place, but we're not going anywhere." I asked her name. "I am Mrs. Gordon. I am from Warsaw and these are my two children." She had a boy who was twenty-one months old and an eleven- or twelve-year-old girl. The second woman was named Reznaykova and the third woman's name was Zosye. Joseph and I looked at them. He was a smart boy; he read my thoughts.

I said, "Wait here until daybreak." Then we left and were fortunate in obtaining food from the beast. We returned to the place of the secret watch, where we had left Mrs. Gordon's group. I told the guard, Meir Laykhtenson (he and his wife are today in Israel), to give the group a fresh loaf of bread and a big piece of pork. I repeated to the group that they should remain there with the secret watch, and I returned to the temporary base and unloaded the food and went to my hut. I waited there until Khyene and Didalyis finished their meal and then I went to talk to them. I had in mind the verse "When the king is in a good mood on account of the wine," then you can talk person to person. As I went to Khyene's hut, Didalyis was coming toward me. He asked if I had arranged accommodations for the people. I told him to come with me to Khyene's hut. There Khyene greeted me with the same question. I told her that the group was presently with the secret watch and that they should be brought here. I asked Khyene, "How can you expect me to send them to their deaths?" I also told her that I would increase my supply-gathering expeditions. Didalyis told me that I had a Jewish heart. Khyene told me I was the good cadet.

"As you wish it!" she said. "Go order someone to bring them here." They brought the three women and the two children. Reznaykova and Zosye were placed with the Second unit, and Mrs. Gordon and her children in the Third Unit. They all survived the war with us. Mrs. Gordon and her children live in America, and Reznaykova and Zosye are living in Israel.

Partisan Heroes

Captain Vasilyenko was appointed to take over my duties in the Third Unit. I returned to the Second Unit. Imke Loybatski remained with the Fourth Unit. Moscow began sending arms and explosives. All the units began performing various types of missions: blowing up trains and cutting telephone wires. Vasilyenko was a military man. He wanted to show that he was doing more than others. He started sending people out to blow up trains. The other units did not hold back. Vasilyenko sent a group of five men to blow up a train. The partisans arrived at the tracks and encountered a group of Lithuanians and Germans. A battle began. Motl Gopstein, a young man from the Third Unit, received a bullet in his stomach. He knew he was going to die. He yelled to his friends: "Escape and I will cover you." He did not want to be captured by the Germans, so he took out his gun and killed himself. He was a heroic individual and a good friend. I knew him well. He was one of the best fighters.*

Vasilyenko of the Third Unit would scout the roads, forests, and surrounding areas by himself. I would often meet him on the roads. For the partisans, weather conditions were not a factor in deciding whether or not to carry out an operation. On one of his excursions, he observed that a telephone line ran alongside the tracks between Lida and Vilna. He came to a junction where the lines went in four directions. I also knew about this junction. There was a special pole on which the wires were twisted in four directions. Vasilyenko sent five partisans to blow it up. Imke Loybatski headed the group. The explosives were already there. They completed their mission; the pole and the wires were blown up. The Germans installed a second pole. The same group went to blow up the second pole and successfully completed their mission. The Germans

---

* Isaac Kowalski, who set the type for the partisan newspaper, noted in his book *A Secret Press in Nazi Europe* (p. 241) that "the story I was setting concerned my good friend the Jewish partisan Motl Gopstein, who had been with a group on a partisan mission to blow up an enemy train. Seeing he was critically wounded and that he was in a trap, he shot himself in the head rather than be taken prisoner."

installed a third pole. Vasilyenko decided to send the same group to destroy the pole a third time. When they arrived they didn't realize that the Germans had mined the area with highly explosive mines. When they began their work, a great explosion occurred, blowing them into pieces. Vasilyenko felt guilty, but no one did anything to him. The staff did not hold him responsible for the mission's failure. In my opinion, his strategy had not been well thought out, and five young and good partisans paid with their lives.

Danke Loybatski, Imke's brother, was a member of the Second Unit. The unit's head scouts discovered that a young Pole was working as a German spy. He lived in a village about 15 kilometers from the forest. Other units also knew about his activities. Each unit wanted to be the first to get their hands on him. Shmuel Kaplinski decided to send some partisans to apprehend him. As leader of this mission, he appointed Danke, who was a member of the Communist Party youth division and close to Khyene. He was very smart and outgoing. They came to the village in the evening and went directly to the house where the spy was staying in order to capture him. Danke was the first to enter and was greeted with a barrage of fire. He was killed, but not by an enemy's bullet. It was from one of his own since another partisan unit was already in the house. They had been waiting for the spy to arrive and mistook Danke for the Pole. They brought Danke back to his unit and buried him with great honor.

THE LOYBATSKI BROTHERS

"Danya [Danke] became commander of the unit's third group Za Pobedu; he was known for his extraordinary daring. He thirsted for revenge; he literally could not sit still and was constantly going out on assignments.

"At the end of December 1943, Danya discovered that one of the Gestapo's top agents was in one of the towns in the area; he got together a group of partisans and set out to hunt down the fascist beast. The German was barricaded in a building that they had under seige; Danya was seriously wounded. He was taken to a camp where his life came to an end.

"Ima [Imke] returned that day after the bitter battle. His brother was interred in the camp. The young man stood at the side of the grave leaning on his rifle, the hot tears running down his cheeks.

"A few days later Ima [Imke] went out with a group of partisans to destroy an enemy telegraph line. One of the telegraph poles turned out to be mined. There was an explosion; Ima and a handful of the fighters were literally blown to pieces.

"Both brothers will sleep forever in peace in the Rudnicki Woods."[13]

Change of Command

One month had elapsed since I was reunited with the Second Unit when news arrived from brigade headquarters that a plane would arrive from Moscow late in the evening. They were going to drop arms, explosives, and equipment for the partisans. The word came down that each regiment must assign a group of men to collect the parachuted ordinance and bring it to staff headquarters.

This was not the first time we had to retrieve supplies from the forest. Headquarters then divided the ordinance among the various units. The evening the ammunition was parachuted, I was away on a mission to obtain supplies. I was frequently on the road. I had a large group of partisans with me for the assignment. In the morning, we came back with wagon loads of food and everything was in order.

There is a Jewish saying: "When someone is due punishment, their senses are taken away." In this instance, that is exactly what happened. **Khyene Borowska, Shmuel Kaplinski**, and Abba Kovner decided to steal some bags of ammunition. They sent a small group out to steal the goods. For some reason, they did not realize that Moscow sent a list of all the goods that were parachuted to us. Our headquarters was also in contact with Moscow by radio. They knew immediately that something dirty had taken place. Our people were the suspected thieves. I personally couldn't understand why they stole the arms.

At headquarters there was a Lithuanian by the name of **Stankevitsh**. He was an old communist and a member of the security unit. He spent his entire life in and out of Polish prisons. He was not a person who believed in mercy. Stankevitsh was assigned by the staff to investigate the theft. He was a very disciplined individual. You couldn't play with him. He came to the platoon and began his investigation. Everyone he questioned told him everything they knew. The people who were on the supply procuring mission with me that night weren't frightened. In fact, we weren't even questioned.

In one day he uncovered all the details. I knew this was the end of the trio of leaders. All three were removed from their positions.

I replaced Kaplinski. Khyene was completely removed from all her responsibilities. No one had faith in her anymore. **Abba Kovner** was replaced by a

KHYENE AND KAPLINSKI
Joseph Harmatz wrote: "Shmulke [Shmuel Kaplinski] was married to Chiena [Khyene] Borowska, one of the leading activists in Vilna, before and during the ghetto years, and then in the underground movement. After he led us out of Vilna through the sewers, Shmulke became a commander of the battalion, 'To Victory [Far'n Nitzahon, For Victory],' and Khyene was the commissar. They remained in Vilna after the liberation, where they still live with their daughter, Ruta (born just after we returned to Vilna from the forests in 1944), her husband and son."[14]

STANKEVITSH was indeed a cruel man. He was known by the nickname "think" because he would scream "think!" at the people he was interrogating. He was the head of a "special investigations unit" that summarily handed down death sentences, which were executed by Russian paratroopers who were deemed loyal.[15]

ABBA KOVNER was sentenced to death as a result of his involvement in this incident, but his sentence was commuted at the last minute. Joseph Harmatz, the nineteen-year-old head of the special unit, may have helped and Kovner himself believed it was Harmatz's intervention that saved his life. There are those who argue that the entire affair was "invented" in order to remove the Jewish leadership of the units. Abrashe was of a very different opinion, as was Harmatz, who believed that the Jewish units had taken the arms. Jewish leaders, Abba included, remained quiet about the "theft."[16]

Lithuanian named Petrites. The majority of the partisans were not angry at the decision. Petrites moved his First Unit five kilometers from us. I remained with the Second Unit and we stayed in the same place until we left the forest for our return to Vilna.*

Gabris, the commissar of the brigade, wanted to know if Kaplinski and Khyene would interfere with my activities. If I had said yes, then he would have transferred them to another place. A few of my friends recommended that I should remove them from the regiment. I told the commissar that if they bothered me, I would inform him and he could then transfer them. I did not have the heart to send Khyene away. She was pregnant. Although she told everybody that she was swollen with water, I knew she was pregnant, and becoming pregnant in the forest was punishable by death. The partisans had a code of strict discipline. If I had agreed with Gobris about removing them from the Jewish detachments and assigning them to a non-Jewish one, they would have been put on trial. They remained with me, but enjoyed no special privileges. A few days before we all left the forest, Khyene gave birth to a girl. She was lucky that a gynecologist, Dr. Moshe Feigenberg, had come to our unit. He was there when she gave birth. He now lives in Israel.

---

* Joseph Harmatz recounted in a telephone interview that when the camp was searched for the missing weaponry, two guns were found in one of the Jewish units.

Chapter 9

"So the woman bore a son and called his name Samson;
and the child grew, and the LORD *blessed him."*

Judges 13:24

"After that day, the priests in all the churches preached that when
the partisans came for food, everyone should all oblige them."

Abrashe Szabrinski

A Vilna Samson the Mighty

I would like to write about a Vilna Jew I met while serving with the partisans.
It was destined that we should both serve in the same unit,
For Victory. When I saw him for the first time, I told my
close friends that he should be called Samson the Mighty,
since that was the impression he gave me. **Tuvya Rubin** was
born in Vilna, but I do not know his later haunts. He worked
as a hauler and manual laborer. He had a large body and the
appearance of a strongman. He had sharp eyes and a smile
on his face. He was an exceptionally kind person and would
help anyone who needed it.

TUVYA RUBIN was also recalled
with admiration by Joseph Harmatz. He remembered Tuvya as
"blessed with natural common
sense and immense physical
strength [he] was one of the finest
human beings I ever met in those
days." Harmatz credits Tuvya with
saving his life when he was entan-
gled in the detonator cord after an
explosion, and the Germans were
shooting wildly from the derailed
train into the surrounding forest.
At the time, Harmatz was a very
young man, around sixteen or seventeen. He also wrote of Tuvya's
almost inhuman ability to drink
samogon, Russian moonshine.[1]

In the unit, he was given the rank of sergeant. What
were his tasks? First, he ensured that three meals a day were
prepared on time. Second, he was responsible for guard duty
and handled the scheduling of the sentry details, which
included the day and night shifts. He was only responsible
to the commander of the regiment. He had a very important post and all the
partisans liked him. Even though he was older than me, he addressed me
formally, though I did not, and he never called me by my name but addressed
me as Comrade Commander. One time I told him, "My name is Abrashe." But

he responded, "To me you are Comrade Commander." He knew I liked him and trusted him completely. I knew he was smart and devoted to the cause. When a group of partisans was assigned to a mission, he was given the orders to prepare them for action. He was not obligated to go on missions, but he would volunteer to accompany the men. He was a disciplined man, courageous and bold. He especially wanted to be part of the missions I led.

As I have written, one of our most difficult duties was to provide food for the fighters. I often went on such missions and met with success. After a while, Tuvya approached me and asked me to take him with me on my next food gathering expedition. He wanted to show everyone that he did not eat for free and that he was not afraid to go into action. I asked him, "Why do you want to go? No one is sending you! You have a very important job!" He did not listen. He wanted to go on the expedition. I agreed to his request. Every time I went on a mission, he went with me. Now, I would like to retell an episode that confirms my giving him the name Samson the Mighty.

At the end of December 1943, I went with a group of forty partisans to obtain food. Tuvya came with me. I was very well informed about the roads and the locations of all the German garrisons, and devised a plan of operation and a way of escape. This time we had fifteen wagons full of produce. The Vilayke River formed a border between the base and our area of operations. In order to shorten our journey, I decided to cross the river not far from the German garrison. All the bridges had been destroyed by fire. Twelve heavily armed Germans were guarding the bridge on the Lida to Vilna highway. About one kilometer from the bridge, the river was a shallow enough for the horses to cross. We reached the Vilayke at 6:00 AM. It was not very wide but it was a deep river with strong currents, and it needed a severe winter in order to freeze over. Summer had its problems, too. On this occasion, it was cold but the water was not frozen.

The Germans were standing guard on the highway. When we reached the point where we wanted to cross, I wasn't sure of the depth of the water. I called Tuvya over and told him that we had to measure the depth of the water. He said that he would do it himself. He crossed the river. The water reached his chest. When he reached the other side, he shouted to us and told us where we could cross. The partisans gathered the wagons and crossed the river at the spot he was showing us. When we had traveled a kilometer away from the river, I ordered the wagons to halt and had a fire made. I wanted Tuvya to warm up and dry himself from the ice-cold water. One of the wagons was loaded with home distilled whiskey that was manufactured by the farmers. We called it **samogon**. I sent one of the partisans to fetch me a liter of it. I gave it to Tuvya and told him to drink it. He started to drink the whiskey and brought the bottle to me. I told him to continue drinking. He asked me: "How much should I drink?"

I said to him, "Drink." This was repeated a few times. Finally Tuvya finished the entire bottle of *samogon*. I had the feeling that he would not become sick from the whiskey, and indeed he did not have a negative reaction. I was sure that the whiskey would prevent pneumonia. He was such a great heroic individual. Another five partisans would have become drunk from sharing the same strong bottle of *samogon*, but not Tuvya. He was a real Samson the Mighty. I made no mistake by calling him that. I am retelling his story out of the greatest respect and highest regard for him. He was a mighty man. He is no longer with us, but his name should never be erased from our memories. Tuvya Rubin, Samson the Mighty of Vilna, his memory should be honored by all of us. He managed to live through the war and then immigrated to Israel. He married and had a son. He died in Israel.

Chaim Yelin

Chaim Yelin organized the Kovno underground. He and a few Kovno partisans came to the Rudnicki Forest in early fall 1943. They had to pass through fields, forests, and filth on a journey of more than 100 kilometers. They did not want to stay permanently, but to know if they could send **more fighters** into the woods. As I have previously written, they were

"**Samogon** is Russian moonshine. It comes in many flavors, is distilled from many ingredients, and is often of near atomic strength. It holds a special place in Russian drinking culture as a kind of Robin Hood of alcohol."[2]

Joseph Harmatz remembers the drink this way: "We could get it from local village peasants, each house had its own recipe they were reluctant to give up, but they were all lethal. Called samogon, which means 'home brewed' – you never knew exactly what had gone into it, neither the level of alcohol it contained nor the amount of poison. Just smelling it made you reel."[3]

MORE FIGHTERS

"Yelin slipped out of the [Kovno] ghetto and traveled...to the Rudnicki Forest near Vilna, where he contacted Soviet partisans. Following the meeting, the JFO [Yidishe Algemeyne Kamfs Organizatsie] agreed to send small detachments of fighters into the Augustow Forest, south of Kovno, to join the partisans and set up bases of operation. All told, almost a hundred members of the JFO escaped from the ghetto in those missions; most were captured or killed by German troops. In spite of these heavy losses, the Jewish underground was still able to bring more than three hundred fighters from the ghetto to the forests, where they joined with Soviet partisans in fighting German troops.

"Yelin, however, did not live to see liberation. On April 6, 1944, while on a mission outside the Kovno ghetto, he was captured after a gunfight with police and turned over to the Gestapo. Fearing mass reprisals against Kovno's remaining Jews, he hid his identity and insisted, even under pain of torture, that he was a Soviet paratrooper. Several weeks later, in early May 1944, Yelin was killed."[4]

already deployed in the forests. Chaim met with Commander Kostia to get permission to send in more Kovno fighters, even though most of them did not have ammunition. Kostia replied that he would not permit anyone in the forest without ammunition. What should Chaim do? The Kovno regiment told him to go and speak with Abrashe. They meant me. He came with a few of his companions. I got to know him. He made a positive impression on me and I found it very interesting to speak to him. He informed me of his mission and the reason he had made contact with me. I asked him why he was so late. He answered that "In Vilna it is never late! The Jews of Vilna live with hope and that is the reason I came."

I said to him. "All the Jews you send me I'll accept. Don't worry about anything, just bring the people." I took out a map and decided where and when he should return. I would meet him with armed partisans. I warned him not to speak about this to anyone. "When you return, everything will be ready for you," I said.

Chaim returned to Kovno. Sometime later, I was told that he was recognized on the streets and killed. There are various versions about how he met his death. Some people say he was shot and others that he committed suicide by cutting his throat. It is a pity that he wasn't able to bring more Jews to the forest. He was a brave and heroic individual, and should be remembered with honor.

An Attack on a German Convoy

The **Rudnicki Forest** had many positive as well as negative attributes. On the positive side, it was large, encompassing an area of roughly 2,500 square kilometers [see additional discussion of the forest in "The Ghetto Gate," chapter 5]. On the negative side, many roads crisscrossed the forest, including the causeway connecting Lida and Vilna, which traversed the entire wooded area. German garrisons, with ten soldiers each, were set up along this road to guard its bridges. They were armed with heavy automatic guns and certain garrisons had artillery cannons.

Yitzhak Arad described some aspects of the RUDNICKI FOREST. "The Rudnicki forests, located about 50 kilometers (31 miles) southwest of [Vilna], have an area of about 2,500 square kilometers (1,533 square miles), and the main [Vilna]-Grodno road runs through it."[5]

My fighting unit, Povyedu (For Victory) [see note on Khyene and Kaplinski, "Change of Command," chapter 8] was situated deep in the forest, but only four kilometers from the highway. Whenever we were sent on a mission, we would have to pass it. To reach the causeway, we had to use a narrow forest road. Two kilometers to the east of this road there was a wooden bridge guarded by a well-armed German garrison. The bridge had no strategic importance so we did not attack it, a fact that pleased the Germans. We performed our activities at night and they carried out their actions by day, including the gathering of food.

One day, a detachment from my unit learned that a large truck laden with food would be passing by guarded by a truck full of well-armed Germans. It wasn't often that they would cross the highway at the same times of day. They would use the road one week and then stay away for two weeks. One week they would travel in the morning and another time in the afternoon. After researching their movements for many weeks, it was established that on a certain day they would be traveling from eight to nine in the morning. I decided to attack the Germans. I did not know their numbers. We had arms, automatic guns and two machine guns that Moscow had parachuted to us. I proposed to the commander of the First Unit that he should assist me with the mission. His name was Petrites Aleytvin. He had replaced Abba Kovner and we got on very well. He assigned me thirty of his fighters and two machine guns. He also participated in the mission. I wanted it to be a complete success. Until we reached our destination, none of the fighters knew what the mission was about or where they were going.

We arrived at the causeway at 4:00 AM with sixty fighters. Fifteen of them were under Petrites's command and occupied the right wing with machine guns. On the left wing, I assigned fifteen partisans to the head of our spy branch, Yitzhak Tshuzshy. I had thirty combatants stationed in the center area. They camouflaged themselves with twigs and grass. The order was given that no one was to move. We heard the trucks. I allowed them to enter the center area, then I shot at them. They were met with a wall of firepower. The trucks came to a halt and all the Germans were killed, among them two officers. We captured two machine guns, forty guns, two automatic sawed-off guns, two revolvers, and a few grenades. They did not have the opportunity to fire one shot. The mission was a complete success without any losses on our side. That afternoon, three big tanks came to retrieve the dead soldiers.

The young fighters of the Vilna ghetto were victorious.

A Righteous Gentile Saves Us from Certain Death

I went on a mission with fifteen partisans. We were headed in the direction of **Olkieniki**. Around five kilometers outside the town, we needed to take a detour in a northern direction. We had to cross a bridge that went over the Vilayke River and reach a certain destination. On our way back, we had to follow the same route. The mission was to try to discover ammunition hidden by certain farmers. We reached our destination without encountering any difficulties. We searched for the ammunition but did not find any. We started on our way back. When we were two kilometers from the bridge, the reconnaissance unit made up of two partisans came running towards us. They said that a farmer wanted to speak to us. They brought him to me and I asked him where he lived. He said that his place was not far from the bridge we had to cross. Then he told us that yesterday, an hour after we crossed the bridge, 200 Germans from the garrison crossed behind us and took up positions waiting for our return.

OLKIENIKI was a small town located about 48 kilometers south of Vilna. It had a population of about 1,100 at the beginning of the twentieth century, but this declined to about 800 around the time of the German occupation. On June 25, 1941, two days after the Nazis entered the area, German bombs caused a fire that destroyed most of the shtetl's small wooden structures. Many of the town's inhabitants fled to surrounding villages. At the end of September 1943, on the eve of Rosh Hashanah, the remaining Jews of Olkieniki were sent to the town of Eishyshock on the other side of the Merkys River, where they were shot.[6]

"They are from the Olkieniki garrison and are well armed with machine guns." Finally he said that he would lead us across the river at a flat spot. I believed him. I observed him while he was talking and truth radiated from him. He took the lead while we were crossing the river. We arrived at our base without mishap. Later we confirmed that if we had used the regular route, crossing the bridge, the Germans would have killed us all. It would have been catastrophic for someone to save us. The righteous gentile saved our lives.

After the war, I retold this story to the leaders of Vilna. The righteous gentile was supposed to receive a medallion and was appointed as representative of the area in which he lived, which included many villages. It is a shame that I do not remember his name, but I can see his countenance now. He was an honest and precious man, as well as a truly righteous person. If he is no longer alive, I would like to state that he should be remembered as an honorable man.

The Shoemaker

Among the hundreds of partisans, there were many types of people. Some were bright and others not so bright; there were good ones as well as not very good ones. There were disciplined partisans and those who were introduced to discipline.

In my regiment, there was a partisan named Meir Volozshni and his wife Fanye, whom he loved very much. He would do anything in his power for her. Meir was a good partisan who often went on missions. Most of the time, he joined groups that went to gather food. When they went on such expeditions, the partisans were also able to take butter, honey, and other delicacies produced in small quantities by the farmers whose homes they visited. They would hide these special food items keeping them for their loved ones. Meir Volozshni also did this. His commander knew about this proclivity, but it did not bother him. The most important aspect of the mission was to bring back plenty of bread, meat, potatoes, and salt. The objective was that the entire community should be well supplied with food. You were allowed to take anything you wanted from the farmers, but not his last cow or his last horse. This was an order that came from Moscow. A partisan was permitted, however, to take the farmer's last pair of shoes. Not only were shoes and boots difficult to obtain, but the partisans' footgear would often rip on account of all the night marches.

As it happened, Meir Volozshni was a shoemaker. As I became aware of the serious shoe situation, I called him into my office. I told him that from then on he would not be going on food gathering missions. Instead, I told him, you will remain at the base and repair your comrades' shoes. I thought he would be very appreciative of his new assignment. He did not take what I said seriously and in fact he told me that he would not repair shoes. He said he would continue searching for food as he had always done.

I knew the reason for his reaction; he wanted to bring back treats for his wife, Fanye. I told him that this was an order. I informed Sergeant Rubin that he was not to assign Meir to any of the units going out on food gathering operations. Then I found out that Meir did not listen. He had gone out on the provisioning detail and refused to repair shoes for the partisans even though they needed them desperately. I ordered him arrested. We placed him in a bathhouse and two partisans guarded him. He had a brother in the Third Unit. I called for him. I spoke to his brother and to his wife about the critical situation regarding the lack of shoes. Fanye already knew about Meir's stubbornness. I gave them half an hour to speak with Meir and tell him that if he didn't obey my orders, I would put him before the firing squad. I meant it. After they talked to him, he agreed to follow orders. He came out with his wife and brother, apologized for his stubbornness, and began repairing shoes for the partisans. He knew I was right and that all the partisans would have backed up the sentence I had pronounced. He is living in the Land of Israel and I am sure he has no resentment toward me.

Three Jewish Brothers

There was a Russian unit camped ten kilometers from the Second Unit on the so-called Long Island, which we called the Lange Vispe or a long piece of land. The Russian unit was made up of paratroopers, people who had been expelled from Russia, escapees from German POW camps, and three Jewish brothers. Their commander was a Russian named Vasya, a lieutenant in the Red Army. They had one fault. A great many of them were extreme drunkards. Also, a minority was poisoned with anti-Semitism. Most of the former prisoners performed very dangerous operations. They would always cross the train tracks of the Vilna/Lida line. Once, when they went on a night mission, they were ambushed by a large contingent of Germans and Lithuanians. They possessed excellent arms and were well-trained soldiers. It was a bitter encounter. The Russians killed a few Germans and then retreated from the battle area. Two of the Jewish brothers took part in the battle. The youngest one, who was about seventeen or eighteen years old, became frightened when the shooting began and fled.

He was the first to arrive at his unit's headquarters. They called him a deserter. He was to be court-marshaled in the morning and would surely be killed for his behavior. One of the brothers secretly left his unit to speak to me. I mounted my horse and very quickly reached his unit. I told the guards I had orders from the brigade's staff commander. They allowed me to enter their headquarters. When I went into the room, Vasya, the commander, had his head down. He knew me very well.

When he saw me, he said that I had come too late. The court-marshal had been concluded and the boy had already been shot. I relayed some very strong words to him in Russian. I also asked him where his logic was. As a military man, he should have known better. "You were dealing with a young boy without military training." I left without saying anything more. Three days later, Vasya went out on a mission not far from the Rudnicki train station with a few partisans. Germans shot at them and Vasya was mortally wounded. When I met some of the fighters later on, they commented that he deserved to die. He had allowed a person to be killed unjustly, and so he was killed. There his life ended. The same opinion was obviously held by the Russian partisans. They wondered how one commander could have so much power on his own.

The three Varshavtshik brothers were also members of the partisans. Hirshke was in the Third Unit and Hilke was in the Second Unit. They were both good partisans. **Leyalke**, a heroic partisan, was a member of a Russian unit. He often took part in the blowing up of trains. He excelled in what he did. The Russians respected him. He would also join spy units. He knew all the roads leading to the villages. One winter day he went to see a gentile to find out if he had news for him. When he returned to his unit on his own, he was shot. There are many rumors, but the truth was never ascertained. Knowing the truth was a tragedy.

LEYALKE

It is probably no coincidence that the brother who was shot was out with a Russian partisan detachment. Abrashe does not say, and in this case he most likely did not know for sure, but the tragedy of Leyalke's death may be that he was killed for being a Jew. This was a frequent practice in the non-Jewish partisan units. It's also possible he was shot because they did not trust him and considered his absence as traitorous.

The Death of My Friend Kostie

In one area of the Rudnicki Forest, there were several villages situated close to one another. Since a great many of the villagers would share important information with the partisans, we were not permitted to take anything from them. This was an order from the staff of the Lithuanian Brigade.

Two units were camped together in the forest. They were comprised mainly of Jews, along with a small number of non-Jews, all from Kovno. The commander was a Lithuanian named Radionov who was a party member. He was not a pleasant man. He never went out on assignments. He had two deputies, one was Vasye, a young lieutenant, and other was Kostie. I did not know his surname. He was a gentleman and had the rank of lieutenant. He was a handsome man with a heroic appearance, and he had a very good nature. He was bold and ambitious, and headed the spy unit. Not far from one of the villages, there was a solitary house occupied by a father, a son, and a daughter. The girl was very pretty. She did not fit the village girl type. Kostie developed a personal relationship with her. He would send her to Vilna with important information. She was ambitious and very clever. I thought of going with him when he would visit her.

On one occasion, I spoke to him about the girl. I told him he should be sure of her allegiance. "She is too intelligent and too smart. She might be a double agent. When she visits Vilna, a German might fall in love with her, and she could be influenced by him." He laughed and answered that he was certain about her honesty and her devotion to him. I replied that he should be smart and perform a proper verification. About six weeks afterwards, she again went to Vilna to bring important news. Instead of bringing news, she brought a group of Germans into the forest. They encircled her house. Kostie and a group of partisans awaited her arrival. Instead of coming in the evening, she and the Germans arrived in the morning. She knew that Kostie would be waiting for her.

The Germans wanted to capture Kostie and the partisans alive. It was 6:00 AM. Shooting broke out. The partisans broke through the German encirclement, but Kostie was mortally wounded. He was very strong and with the help of his comrades they were able to flee deeper into the forest. The Germans failed because they allowed fear to overcome them. They found themselves in partisan territory and fled from the forest. The partisans brought Kostie to the base. He was severely wounded. The commander, Romanov, knew of all his adventures and had to report all his actions and their objectives to the brigade staff. Two days later Kostie died of his wounds. This had a terrible effect on all the partisans. The brigade staff ordered Romanov to initiate an energetic investigation. Guards were placed everywhere.

Two days after Kostie's death, the father, the son, and the daughter were arrested and interrogated. Under extreme torture, Kostie's lover admitted that she also had a romance with a German and told him everything she knew. She really didn't know too much. She did not know how many partisans were operating in the Rudnicki Forest. The father and son admitted that they knew of her doings. All three were sentenced to death. Romanov, the commander, had no mercy since Kostie had been his right hand. All three traitors' hands and feet were tied with wire. They were thrown into a prepared ditch and buried alive. This was the death meted out to those who caused the death of the hero Kostie, the head of reconnaissance for the Kovno Unit.

Military Punishments: Koniuchy

As I have already said, obtaining food was one of the most dangerous jobs for the partisans. This was true for many reasons. First, many of the villages were located at a great distance from our base. Second, they were near German garrisons. These garrisons were of different sizes. They had twenty, forty, or even more soldiers, and were also armed with the best weapons. The farmers were also well aware of the roads the partisans used to enter their villages in the darkness of night. The Germans had given arms to the villagers so they could shoot at us when we approached.

One such village was **Koniuchy**. It was a large, rich village with a population of 300 families located about 20 kilometers from our base in the woods. The villagers shot at us on two occasions. Luckily there were no fatalities, but I wasn't able to bring back food either. To begin a war with them made no sense. We did not know their numbers. Even if we were able to beat them, it wouldn't increase the success of our food gathering missions.

Isaac Kowalski corroborates that **KONIUCHY** was friendly to the Germans, adding that it became a bigger problem as time went on so that the partisans had to take action.

Later, when "we had to go through Koniuchy we did not encounter any sniper shots, because it was like crossing through a cemetery."[8]

After getting shot at a second time, I told Khyene, who was still commissar at that time, that we should go to the brigade staff headquarters and approach the chief of staff, **Yurgis**, and tell him that strong measures should be initiated to overcome the present situation. We went to Yurgis and delivered our report. He then asked me my opinion on the matter. I told him that "The village of Koniuchy must be destroyed. This will be an example to the other villages." He answered that he couldn't decide on his own. "This evening I will contact Moscow and ask them for their approval for such an action. I cannot take such a responsibility on myself. In the evening we'll contact Moscow by radio. Tomorrow we will receive a reply."

YURGIS

Years later, Abrashe wrote: "By profession, Yurgis was a teacher. After the war he became the editor of the largest Lithuanian newspaper in Vilna. He visited America a few times; in 1980 he came there to attend a convention of writers and editors. A small group of partisans met him. The reception was hosted by one of our own partisans, Nuysye Loybatski Delugiy.... When we met we hugged and kissed each other. Then he asked me if I remembered Koniuchy. 'Do you remember when I told you I needed Moscow's approval? I told you a lie. It was necessary for me to lie. I knew you were right about the mission and I was in total agreement with you.' This is what he shared with me all those years after the event. Yurgis, whose real name was Henri Ziman, was a precious man. He possessed all the beautiful attributes. He died on July 15, 1985. He was given one of the grandest funerals. He was escorted with great honor to his everlasting rest to be remembered with honor."

Khyene and I were not happy with his decision, but there was nothing else to do but wait. Yurgis was the commander of the brigade. Next day he sent a messenger to us with news that Moscow had given permission for a punitive action against the village. He appointed one of the senior lieutenants by the name of Vanke to lead the mission. Each unit had to assign twenty men, so that 200 partisans would be taking part in the operation. I did not go since I was sent to bring food and would be traveling in a different direction. I knew the plan of action. We all knew about the village of Koniuchy, the number of villagers who lived there, as well as the number of houses. We also knew that there was a river on the west side of the village. It was not very wide, but it was very deep. We were also aware that a German garrison was located ten kilometers from the village.

The plan and the orders were well thought out. The 200 partisans were to reach the village about an hour before daybreak. That was when the Germans guarding Koniuchy would leave and head back to their garrison. They knew that partisans didn't come to search for food during the day. Our men waited for the moment the Germans left. The order was that no booty whatsoever should be taken from the village. The mission was to destroy and burn everything we saw. Twenty warriors were placed in the area where the Germans might enter the village to render assistance.

The operation lasted about three hours. In that time, everything was wiped off the face of the earth. It was a total success. There were no partisan casualties.* Yurgis was a clever and precise person. He sent out groups of people to find out how the other villages had reacted. The situation changed completely. It was imperative to carry out this severe task. It was a question of life or death. The partisans required three things to survive: arms, food, and shoes for their feet. These were a must.

---

* Isaac Kowalski (*A Secret Press in Nazi Europe*, p. 279) described the action against Koniuchy in detail: "The brigade staff decided to remove the cancer that was growing on the partisan body…when we were closing in on our destination I saw that the partisans were coming from all directions from various detachments…. Our detachment got the order to destroy everything that was moving and burn the village down to its roots. At the exact hour and minute all partisans from all four corners of the village started pouring rifle and machine gun fire, with incendiary bullets, into the village. This caused the straw roofs of the houses to catch fire. The villagers and the small German garrison answered back with heavy fire, but after two hours the village with the fortified shelter was completely destroyed…."

After that day, the priests in all the churches preached that when the partisans came for food, everyone should oblige them. And so it was! We knew that in a few months we would be relocating, but we did not know exactly where. After the Koniuchy mission, we remained in the forest another three months.

The Death of Seventeen Partisans from the Kovno Units

As I already said, Radionov, the commander of the Kovno units never participated in any operations. His two deputies did go out on those missions, however. They were the leaders of the reconnaissance unit, Kostie and Vasye, a young Lithuanian lieutenant. Vasye proposed to initiate an attack on the German garrisons in the village of Rudnicki. There were three villages with the name Rudnicki. There was Rudnicki Station on the train line between Vilna and Lida. Sixteen kilometers east of the station there was a fort that the Germans used to protect a bridge, Rudnicki Bridge. The village of Rudnicki was situated eight kilometers from the fortress and thirty well-armed Germans were garrisoned there. They employed a great many of the villagers, who felt secure in their belief that no partisans would bother them.

Young Vasye decided to attack the village and perhaps drive out the Germans. He made a mistake by not investigating their strength. He chose to attack them when they were at their stations, planning the attack for 6:00 AM. He had a group of sixty partisans. They were a well-armed and powerful force. Regretfully, on the day of the attack they encountered terrible resistance and lost seventeen partisans in the first ten minutes of the battle. They had to retreat or they would all have been killed by the Germans. They weren't able to remove the dead from the battlefield. It was a calamity, especially for the Kovno Jewish units. All seventeen fatalities were Jews from Kovno. The brigade staff investigated the operation. Lieutenant Vasye was sentenced to be shot. The sentence was carried out. Discipline was severe in the partisan groups.

The First Unit, led by the Lithuanian commander Petrites, was located six kilometers from the village. My unit was positioned a distance of three kilometers from them. Each commander had permission to lead his group into battle whenever he thought it was necessary. The commander would take full responsibility for the mission.

I decided I was going to pay them back. I sent out our *razvedka* [see note on *razvedka* in "Reconnaissance," chapter 8] or spy unit to find out where the cows were led from the village to pasture, as well as the distance from the pasture to the village, and from the village to the forest. They brought back all the information. I decided to capture a few of their cow herders as well as their entire herd, and bring them to our territory. I sent out three partisans, Leon Tshibuk, Abrashe Tshuzshy, and Kalye Akhmatov. All three were good and capable fighters. They reached the herders from the direction of the village. There was a large herd of animals attended by four people. They stared in disbelief when they saw the partisans coming from the village rather than the forest. The partisans took the men and the beasts, and brought them to our forest.

I came to the area with a group of twenty partisans. Then I sent one of the herders into the village to bring back some of the farmers who owned the cows that had been taken to the forest. A few of them met with me and I put forth the stipulation that for every cow I gave back to them, they would in turn provide me with other rations, including potatoes and produce, for an indefinite period of time in the future. But I did not return all their cows. If someone owned three cows I gave back two and kept one.

The discussion went on for hours. The Germans, the villagers' protectors, did not move from their positions inside the village, even as its inhabitants brought us many wagons with supplies. Commander Petrites was a little jealous of me, but he couldn't do anything about it. We gave him a few of the cows and remained friends as before this operation. The village learned a lesson. All of this occurred in June 1944, about a month before we left the forest.

This is the way it happened. Everything I have written is deeply engraved in my memory.

The Nine-Year-Old Spy

One time a Christian woman with a nine-year-old boy came to see me. I asked her to identify herself and she said that she was a partisan from **Misha**'s group. The partisans of one group would visit other groups so they could get to know one another. Later I met Misha and asked him about this woman. He said that she was the wife of a Red Army soldier who was either imprisoned or dead. She had fled from the Germans

MISHA was the Russian who discovered Abrashe and his partner Shulamit when they first escaped from Vilna and were wandering around in search of the Rudnicki Forest. At that time, he took Abrashe's gun in exchange for food [see "The Sewers," chapter 6].

so as not to be captured and sent to Germany as a slave. Misha had therefore accepted her into his unit. At one time, she had been a beautiful woman.

I visited Misha's unit a few times and noticed that she behaved like any other member of the unit but that her son did not behave like a nine-year-old boy. Both of them visited my unit several times. I noticed that the boy was interested in guns. He would tap the ammunition and speak with the partisans like no other nine-year-old I had ever seen. He showed interest in everything he saw. I met Misha and told him that he should watch them.

He told me not to be a fool. Sometime later, around the month of May, I was on a mission with a group of partisans. We were going to a certain village and traveling in the direction of Vilna. I had ten men with me. We were to enter the village, but we encountered shooting while still in our territory. I realized that some of our partisans were under fire. We drew in closer to the village. White Poles had intercepted Misha and his group of partisans. One of his men was already dead and Misha was shot in both his feet. He saw me. He pleaded with me that I should not leave him there. The partisans made a bed out of boards and twigs to carry him away. We brought him back to the base. His group carried him back, and my group kept watch. I did not want to fight the Poles because I did not know their numbers. I knew that both our groups together only added up to eighteen people, and that one of his fighters was already killed and Misha was severely wounded. In the morning a group of his partisans brought back the fighter who had been killed. At the base, Misha was lying down and a doctor from another Russian group was tending to him.

I came to see him a few times. One day while I was visiting him, his unit went on a mission and he remained at the base. At this point he was walking on crutches. All of a sudden there was a tumult in the base. Riders on horseback were demanding that the partisans encircle the exit to the forest. They were searching for the Christian lady and her nine-year-old boy. They had stolen ammunition from Misha's unit and were missing. They had run away.

The partisans captured them as they were leaving the forest. The little bastard shot at us with Misha's automatic. The boy was shot and the woman was captured. She divulged all her secrets. She and the small bandit had taken part in a spy course given by the Germans. Their mission was to uncover the various types of ammunition employed by the partisans and to ascertain how many partisans there were. She told us everything. She received her just reward. She was shot dead. Misha recuperated and again went on missions. He returned my revolver. He admitted to me that I had been a keen observer to uncover the traitor.

Chapter 10

"Henceforth the word German means to us the most terrible curse.
From now on the word German will trigger your rifle. We shall not
speak anymore. We shall not get excited. We shall kill. If you have not
killed at least one German a day, you have wasted that day."[1]

Ilya Ehrenburg

A Meeting with Ilya Ehrenburg

On July 13, 1944, the Jewish partisans of Vilna united with the Red Army. We fought together for the liberation of Vilna. Many of the partisans served as scouts for the Red Army, informing them about the best positions to take in order to encircle Vilna. Inside the city, thousands of Germans put up a bitter fight against the Red Army and the partisans. After they were encircled, the murderers were forced to surrender. Hundreds of Nazis corpses were strewn about the city. Most of them were members of the SS. The heat was intense and the smell of the decaying bodies poisoned the air. We captured 8,000 of the fascist enemy. The partisans may have fought together with the Soviet army to liberate Vilna, but it was empty of its precious Jewish population, and looked like one enormous graveyard.

We knew what was happening on the front and that the defeat of the Nazis was imminent. On July 12, 1944, we received orders to be ready to travel to Vilna and join the Red Army. When Vilna was liberated the next day, we were there. We met the first Russian tanks. The first **tank commander** we met was a Jew. He was happy to greet us and we were gratified to meet him as well as all the other soldiers we encountered there.

Around the city of Vilna there were hundreds of dead Nazis lying on the

TANK COMMANDER
The Russian tank commander's name was Yonah Degen. Upon entering Vilna, he encountered a group of ragtag looking soldiers who were all speaking Yiddish, which, as he later wrote, sounded to him like the voice of the Messiah. He had met up with the Jewish partisans. In turn, Dinah Porat writes that Abba Kovner took the fact that "a Yiddish-speaking Jew came in a tank to the ghetto and liberated it" as a sign from heaven.[2]

ground. Most of them were members of the SS. An awful smell hovered over the city. The partisans together with the Russian army liberated Vilna. We captured 8,000 of the enemy. And while Vilna may have been liberated, it was empty of its precious Jewish population, and appeared as one great graveyard.

On July 14, a Jeep arrived at the place where I was quartered. A fellow partisan, a former POW who had served with us, jumped out of the vehicle. He ran toward me and said that our friend **Ilya Ehrenburg** was coming to see us. Then a car arrived and a man in civilian clothes appeared before us. He was wearing a cap on his head and had a camera on his arm. It was Ehrenburg, and behind him were two officers from the Russian Security Forces.

ILYA EHRENBURG was a famous Soviet Jewish journalist and writer known primarily for his coverage of three wars: WWI, the Spanish Civil War, and WWII. *The Black Book of Russian Jewry*, which he wrote, is an important historical work containing firsthand accounts of eastern European Jewry under the Nazi regime. The book was censored by the Soviets for many years.[3]

The majority of my fighters were on the base and I ordered them to assemble into two rows. This was done immediately with military exactness. I recognized Ehrenburg's name. We had read his articles in the newspapers. His words, his thoughts, his supreme talent with the pen always hit the mark. Millions of people answered his call and fought against the fascist, bestial murderers who were finally conquered. Now we had the opportunity to meet with this great personality who possessed a Jewish heart and a love for the Jews. We gave him our complete attention and expressed our feelings for him. I introduced myself, since I was in charge of our unit and its representative. Ehrenburg addressed everyone with the Russian greeting of "comrade." Along with the other partisans, we went into a house where we could talk to him. He recorded our statements in his notebook. Then we took pictures. A picture of Ehrenburg and I always hung in his study in Moscow, the room in which he wrote his important works. Chaim Zaydelson, a former partisan who presently resides in Vilna, told me this.

When we were returning to the automobile, Ehrenburg squeezed my hand and told me how proud he was of me. I totally ignored the two officers accompanying him. Ehrenburg, the great writer, received all of our attention. The two security officers observed us and obviously noted all of our actions. I was sure their report on the gathering was read in Moscow behind the Kremlin's walls. This was their mission: to watch this great writer, this great propagandist, this great talent who contributed to the downfall of the enemy. They also had to watch Ehrenburg the citizen. Unfortunately, this is the system of every dictator and he was well aware of this situation. In both of these aspects, as a writer and a citizen, Ehrenburg understood to the core that he was Jewish. We all should honor his memory.

It upsets me to no end that many Jews had a poor opinion of Ehrenburg, including two journalists, Ben-Tzion Goldberg and Yakov Goldshteyn, who wrote for the Jewish press. They asked very puzzling questions about him, such as how did he manage to remain alive during the Stalinist era liquidation of Soviet writers. They were not able to evaluate all he did for the Soviet Union. He was well known to the war leaders, marshals, generals, and to the millions of officers and soldiers in the Soviet army. He wrote the popular article "I Accuse" at the time the Red Army was attacking Berlin, in which he demanded that Stalin **treat the Germans** as they had treated the Russians. He spoke and wrote with the experience of Jewish anguish. When he entered a city along with the Russian army, he found it empty of Jews. In Vilna, where 60,000 Jews had once lived, he found a few hundred partisans. His heart was bleeding in

> **TREAT THE GERMANS**
>
> Ehrenberg championed the Soviet struggle against the Nazis and among other statements, is credited as saying: "From now on the word German will trigger your rifle. If you have not killed at least one German a day, you have wasted that day.... If you do not kill the German, he will kill you. If you cannot kill your German with a bullet, kill him with your bayonet.... Do not count days; do not count miles. Count only the number of Germans you have killed. Kill the German – this is your old mother's prayer. Kill the German – this is what your children beseech you to do. Kill the German – this is the cry of your Russian earth. Do not waver. Do not let up. Kill." [4]

pain. Stalin answered him in an article entitled "A Person on His Back You Don't Hit." One Jewish writer by the name of Shnyderman, who wrote for the *Jewish Daily Forward*, came out with an article supporting Ehrenburg. Shnyderman also praises Ehrenburg in the book he wrote about him. He was the only person with wisdom and logic.

After the War

When the partisan regiments disbanded, each of us wanted to put our lives in order. The war was still going on, but we all wanted to avoid army service. To do so, it was necessary to take up a vocation that assured you would not be drafted into the army. I found a job as a railroad worker and became part of the staff of a Lithuanian Soviet train station. The base provided food for all the railway and white-collar workers.

I had many Jews working under me. My bookkeeper, Pavel, was Jewish. He came from Vilna. The other Jews were Solonuyits, Rudniyik, Yankel Glazman,

Kulbis Vinter, and Moshe Puzeritski. They all lived through the Holocaust. They lost everything, but life must continue. A person is just a person, so he temporarily forgets the shocking experiences. Each of us would on occasion express some words of wisdom or tell a joke. But Moshe Puzeritski never laughed; he was always earnest and sad. One time I asked him, "Why have I never seen you laugh or felt that you were happy that you lived even though you went through harrowing moments?"

Even though I was younger than he was, he was always deferential to me and spoke to me with respect. He responded to my question. "Abrashe," he said, "I want to tell you something."

I responded, "So tell me."

"When we used to leave the ghetto on our own to go to work at six o'clock in the morning, I would take my son to a farmer. This was considered work. We would buy food products and bring them back into the ghetto. One morning, I was taking my son to the farmer. My son was eleven years old and taller than me. We encountered two Gestapo soldiers. They probably were returning from partying the night before. They headed straight toward us and started bothering us. They said that one of us must die. I said, 'Take my son.' They took him and shot him instantly."

This is what Puzeritski told me himself. **Sutskever** also writes about this incident. He stated that the Gestapo told the child to run and then shot him in the back. He does not mention that the father gave the son over to the Gestapo. When he completed his story, I responded, "As long as you live I won't tell anybody your story." Moshe lived all his life with a wounded soul and a pained conscience.

AVROM SUTSKEVER was born in Smorgon, Lithuania, a town not far from Vilna. An accomplished poet, he was a member of the *Young Vilne* writers and artists group before the war. After the Nazi invasion, Sutskever was sent to the Vilna ghetto with his young wife where his mother and new-born son were murdered. In 1943, he fled the ghetto with the FPO to the Russian partisans just prior to the FPO's escape through the sewers. After the war, he helped Ilya Ehrenberg compile and edit *The Black Book of Russian Jewry*, and wrote a section on Vilna.[5]

Once, when we assembled for a Vilna memorial service, I saw Moshe again. When he saw me he turned white as snow and his hands began to shake. I greeted him and said, "I will keep the promise I made to you." Since today he is not among the living, I am permitted to tell his story. This was one of the most shocking tragedies that occurred during the terrible period of Hitler. There were a lot of these occurrences. Mothers gave away their children in order to live, but on most occasions they accompanied their children to their deaths.

The Train Explosion

The office and my base of operation were located not far from the Vilna train station. Trains coming from Lida, Konigsberg, and Kovno would stop there. My office was 200 meters from the train tracks. From my window, I was able to observe the trains that were passing. Working with me in the office was Yankel Glazman and a Jew named Avraham. I forgot his surname. He was from Minsk and his wife and six children lived there. All of a sudden, we heard the crash of two trains. We looked out the window and saw that a fire had broken out in one of the trains. We began filling up buckets of water in order to extinguish the flames.

A Russian lieutenant was running in front of us with a gun in his hand. He yelled at us to get away because in a few seconds the bombs on the train would start exploding. We ran back and hid behind the wall of a burned-out brick building. I stood by the wall, and Yankel Glazman and the Jew from Minsk stood opposite me about a meter apart. All of a sudden, a horrific explosion occurred. The wall where we were standing crumbled and caved in on all three of us. They fell under my feet. My head was split. The ruins of the wall covered almost half my body. Blood was flowing from my head. I felt the two people under me moving, but I couldn't help them. They died under my feet beneath the rubble. I started screaming loudly. A few people ran to me and began removing the debris. I lost consciousness and came to in a military hospital. I was given fourteen stitches. They wanted me to remain in the hospital, but I left to go home. On the way I became dizzy. I held on to a wall and continued walking. All of a sudden I saw a former partisan of mine. His name was Blyakher. He grabbed a wagon from a passing farmer and took me home.

It was a horrific explosion that killed 2,000 people and left many wounded. It shattered most of the windows in Vilna. Doors and windows in an area of ten square kilometers were broken. The next day, a special commission came from Moscow to investigate the tragedy. What happened at the station? One train had workers who were repairing the lines. The second train, with military ordinance on board, was coming from the direction of Lida. It was carrying bombs and some cars contained 50 tons of dynamite each. It was discovered that the military train's brakes were not functioning and couldn't bring the train to a halt. Later on, people were saying that the train was sabotaged, but no one knew who did it.

Another Mission

The partisans from Vilna were liberated on July 14, 1944, but the war was still going on and only ended in May 1945. The Soviets mobilized all the young men from the freshly liberated territories, but we wanted to settle down and stay out of the army. Later on we were informed that the capture of Berlin cost hundreds of thousands of lives. One day when I was walking on Zavalna Street, a Russian military man with the rank of major, who was serving in the counter espionage unit, followed me. He caught up with me and put his hand on my shoulder. He asked me if I was Commander Abrashe and I replied that I was Abrashe. He didn't frighten me since I felt that I was a legitimate citizen of Vilna. Then he said, "I have a mission for you."

"What is the mission?" I asked.

"I can't tell it to you at the moment. I want you to come to our headquarters tomorrow and then we will tell you everything."

I said, "OK," and he gave me the address of the headquarters. In the morning, I arrived there and two colonels were seated at a table. The major came in and greeted me in a friendly manner as if he had known me for long time. One of the colonels took out a piece of paper and studied it. He turned to me and said, "The staff of the partisan brigade gave us your name. We know all about you. We selected you to carry out an important mission. We will assign you a high rank and give you forty men, two of them radio operators. We will give you a short course and then drop you off in **Konigsberg**. You will report on the movements of the German forces. You will wear German uniforms and this will be one of the most important sources of information for our fighting units."

KONIGSBERG was the capital of East Prussia, the easternmost area of German settlement, which was separated from greater Germany by the so-called "Polish Corridor" that gave Poland access to the Baltic Sea. The East Prussians were early and avid supporters of Hitler. There was a massive flight of Germans ahead of the Soviet Army, which destroyed the city. The Soviets renamed it Kaliningrad, and expelled the Germans.[6]

I began to feel a cold sweat over my whole body. I knew right away this was a suicide mission. I then said to the officer, "I will tell you something. I have a wife and a child. I believe I already survived Hitler. I served my fatherland with great diligence and devotion." Then I went to the wall where a large map was hanging. I showed him the spots where the paratroopers would make their jumps. "When you drop me in Konigsberg, there will be a German by every tree," I said.

This was the reality of the matter. They knew I was right. The colonel told me to return tomorrow at the same time. I did not tell my dear wife anything. I returned in the morning. I couldn't fall asleep that night. My common sense told me to be firm and oppose their orders. I had nothing to lose. I had a feeling that the mission would do me in. It would be my death sentence.

The next morning the same major and the same colonels greeted me. They were smiling. I knew this was my day of judgment. It was a matter of life or death. They tried to convince me that it was a great honor to accept such an assignment. They needed someone with my credentials. I mentioned to the colonel that I had a very responsible job, which came with assurances that I would not be drafted into the army, meaning that I was exempt from conscription.

"We know everything. We want you to volunteer for the mission."

I replied, "I will not volunteer, but if you mobilize me then I must go." They realized that I would not be convinced by their words. The colonel told me that I could go home. He also said if they needed me then they would call me. I left them in a gloomy mood. I didn't believe they would leave me in peace. Weeks passed and they didn't call me. Months later I found out that they sent a unit of forty individuals and only four survived the mission. They were shot out of the sky. It was just as I had foreseen. I also discovered that it was Captain Vasilyenko who had ensured my survival [see note on Captain Vasilyenko in "A New Captain," chapter 8, and see "Partisan Heroes" in chapter 8]. After we retook Vilna, he worked in the office of the staff headquarters.

Appendix

Interview Given by Abrashe Szabrinski
to Yad Vashem, November 1971

I was born in the shtetl of Seltz on May 15, 1914. The shtetl is located between Brisk and Baranovich, not far from Kartuz-Bereza.

At one time, the shtetl of Seltz was one of the nicest living areas. The well-known Vilna Gaon was born in Seltz. Important businessmen operated in the shtetl, as well as craftsmen. It was also a center for culture. Before WWI, the Yeshiva Committee of the Grodno gubernia was located there. As years went by, Seltz became smaller and smaller, while Kartuz-Bereza grew and flourished.

At the time of my birth, there weren't many Jews there, but there was a Jewish culture, a worldly civilization, and Jewish and general studies. I was the only one of my six siblings who was enrolled in the schools of Pruzhany and Bereza. I was the oldest child, and I received a worldly and Jewish cultural education. All my brothers and sisters were given only a Jewish education. My father was a worker and a salesman. We experienced good times and bad times. The family would have had a wonderful existence if it weren't for the outbreak of WWII, and Hitler's fascism. Our family was educated. The family would have blossomed due to our Jewish education, but all was destroyed.

Are you able to give over the social life of the shtetl?
There was a social life in the shtetl. There was a large synagogue. It was too large for the Jewish population. There was also a small beit midrash (study hall). There was also a school of general studies. We had a library containing fifteen thousand books – this was unusual for a shtetl of our size. The shtetl had a rabbi, and a slaughterer. The Jews were Torah scholars. We observed Jewish holidays and practiced Jewish laws and customs as well as being aware of the world at large. There existed national organizations as well. The majority

97

of them were Zionist in spirit. I myself was first an officer in the Betar branch of our shtetl, and later a work official in kibbutzim in Kosow-Poleski and in Iwacewicze. The Jewish boys and girls wanted to settle in Israel. All these dreams were destroyed because of the Holocaust.

According to your evaluation, how many Jews lived in the shtetl?
Not a lot! About a hundred families. In the latter years, these families were only able to exist with the help of their relatives in America – sons, daughters, brothers, sisters and uncles.

The focus of employment in the shtetl was the use of one's hands: shoemakers, tailors, carpenters, blacksmiths, locksmiths and grocery men. All of the businesses were in Jewish hands. Not only did the Jews observe the Sabbath, but the gentiles observed the Jewish Sabbath as well – the Jewish holidays created a holy environment, since there was a complete shutdown of businesses.

I believe there were three thousand gentile families in Seltz. The Christian families were dependent on the Jews. The shtetl had regular market days, when business was transacted. Salesmen would come from other places, even from larger towns, to take part in Market Day. They would buy cows, sheep, fowl and fruit. It was a shtetl that conducted a lot of business activities.

The shtetl also had income from those who bought lumber. They bought wood from the nearby forests of the Rozshinoyer Forest. The Rozshinoyer Forest would later play an important role as a refuge for hundreds of partisans – from Pruzhany, Rozshinoy, Iwacewicze, Kosow and a handful from Telz. Unfortunately, very few were able to survive.

Can you share a story of the shtetl?
I know very little about the shtetl. I never came across any unique stories about its development. I think that the shtetl came into being when Jews received permission from the East European governments to enter Poland. Therefore, Seltz was one of the oldest in Poland. I believe that the shtetl has a history as one of the great cities, because its population matched other great cities.

Until WWII, were there any historical buildings in Seltz?
Historical buildings?! The synagogue was one – the Teltsher shul. The Jews called it the nicest shul in the Grodno District. It was the Great Synagogue!

Aside from this great synagogue, there were also two great study halls. They were destroyed by fire. The walls of the synagogue remained from previous wars. The shtetl was very strategic as well, due to the importance of the Yashalde River. They always prevented the attacking and marching armies from entering the shtetl. Great artillery duels occurred. The city burned down many times, but the walls of the synagogue always remained standing. The shul was rebuilt and was of the great structures that the city possessed.

What was the relationship between Poles and Jews?

In general, Anti-Semitism was not widespread. There were many White Russians in the shtetl, as well as other minorities. The Poles were not in the majority. The Jews reaped benefits, since they were just one minority among other minorities.

Who were the prominent personalities of the city?
Who was the last rabbi?

The last rabbi that I remember was Rabbi Yosef Wilamovsky. He came from the shtetl of Trestina. It was situated near Vilna. He had two sons. One was Rabbi Zushe Wilamovsky who lives in Bnei Brak. The second son, Rabbi Meir Cohen, is the rabbi of the Slonimer shul in NY.

Why is the name of the second son Cohen and not Wilamovsky?

I do not know with certainty. I believe that when he was traveling through Russia, then Shanghai, to reach America, he probably had to change his name.

Who was the last president of the community?

We really did not have a community leadership as such. We had important personalities that represented the shtetl. They were David Segal, a teacher; Aharon Kaplan; Meir-Hayim Rubinshteyn; and Yisroel Aharon Furman, my mother's uncle. He was one of the most prominent. He was a scholar and a singer. There were worldly Jews such as Yeshaya Bukhalter and Moshe Langbard. They were the first casualties by German hands – the Germans first rid themselves of the Jewish leaders. All of the Jews lived in harmony. The shtetl was small and everybody knew each other.

I think Seltz was unusual because there existed a harmonious living environment.

Where did you learn during your youth?

I learned by Rabbi David Segal. There was a Talmud Torah in Bereza and then in Pruzhany. Afterwards, I was driven to locksmithing. I went away to learn the trade. Then I found work building sawmills for a large and wealthy locksmithing firm named RogMil. I worked there for many years, with a Jewish-Russian engineer named Mishe Kanamov.

I wanted to travel to Israel, so I went to a Polish kibbutz. It was a revisionist kibbutz, located in Kosow and in Iwacewicze. I was devoted to Betar. I cannot say that I was 100 percent overwhelmed with Betar's philosophy. My aim was to reach Israel, which was the aim of thousands of others who did not make it.

In what year were you mobilized into the Polish army?

I was mobilized into the Polish Army in 1936. I served in the Eighth People's Heavy Artillery. I was the only Jew in the unit of NCOs. One Jew among hundreds of gentiles! And I excelled! On the holidays, I was the Jew who brought the other Jewish personnel to the synagogue. There were a few hundred Jews that I would take to the synagogue in Torun.

Right before the war, I was released from duty and came home. In my shtetl, there was no work available. I traveled to Kobrin in search of work, and from there on to Baranovich.

When the war broke out, I was again called to serve in the Polish Army. I was not afforded the opportunity to go to the front lines. I was assigned to the Ninth People's Heavy Artillery Unit. We were hit and bombed on the way to the front, and the officers and soldiers fled to safety.

I and a group of soldiers somehow landed in the shtetl of Kovel. It was located between Brisk and Rivne. There I met up with Jews of great stature. One was Rabbi Eliyahu Mazor of Warsaw. I had the honor of providing him and his son with bread. At that point we became partisans, and searched for bread from the gentiles.

From Kovel I was supposed to travel to Brisk, but we were unable to enter Brisk because of the conflict there. We wondered: Does Brisk belong to the Russians or to the Germans? So a group of us from Rozshinoy, Pruzhany and Bereza continued on foot.

We arrived in the shtetl of Kobryn on Yom Kippur, 1939. We entered the synagogue and the rabbi gave us a dispensation to eat. We had been traveling on foot, day and night, for three days without any food. We spent the entire Yom Kippur in Kobryn and in the evening, after Yom Kippur, we went with Soviet trucks in the direction of Bereza. I had arrived home!

Our shtetl was in a state of silence. The Soviet power had arrived and had ground everything to a halt.

My two younger brothers, Binyamin and Laybl, traveled to Baranovich for work. Binyamin was a tailor and Laybl was a baker. They worked there and earned good money. They wrote to me that I should travel there.

I did travel to Baranovich and I met up with them. I was able to find work as a locksmith at Yosel Yevitshn's sawmill. I lived with my brothers until April 1941, when they were mobilized into the Soviet Army.

I was called into the Red Army. They removed all Polish NCOs. As I later learned, we were to be the vanguards that would be stationed at the front lines. I was in the Red Army but was freed from the duty. However, three weeks before war broke out, I was recalled.

In Baranovich I reported that I had arrived as a member of the Red Army. In a short while, the war broke out. When I came to the commissariat, to whom we had to report, they assigned eighty men to me. They thought that I was the oldest of them. I was to bring this group to the 504 People's Unit in Lesnaye. I asked the Soviet authorities for a vehicle or two. They responded that they had no vehicles and that we must go on foot.

We reached there by foot. There were only two officers and three soldiers at our destination. They told me that the unit that we were to join was already in Minsk and we must return to our place of origin.

The return trip took triple the time. On the way back, we were bombed. We encountered many casualties but not from my unit. I realized that we wouldn't be able to join the unit, and told my men that they should flee to wherever they thought best. I tore up all of the official documents.

I arrived in Baranovich and met up with all of the Jews in the ghetto. The next day, the Germans arrived and it became an official ghetto. Normal ghetto life was the order of the day. We began going to work. The ghetto became more congested day to day. We were unable to travel anywhere. I worked at the sawmill. I was no longer a locksmith but a mechanic. I worked with Israel Berkowitz (today in Israel), Motele Zshukhovitski (killed) and Berel Rabinovitch (killed). We would lead horses and the wagons, loaded with blocks of wood, to the sawmill. We accepted this work as a means of bartering with the gentiles. We also planned to hear what developments were taking place. In this way, we knew more news than others.

We worked in this manner until Purim of 1942. On the eve of Purim, the ghetto was surrounded by the Germans. Right away, we began to suffer. We called all the Jews from the sawmill to discuss our reaction to the new events. Should we re-enter the ghetto, or should we flee?

The German who administered the ghetto was an invalid. He had been wounded at the front. He was also quite a liberal individual. He assured us that those who worked would receive proper documents, would be respected and would not be bothered. We decided to sleep in the sawmill and not to enter the ghetto.

In the morning of Purim 1942, the great slaughter of the Baranovich ghetto took place. I do not know the exact toll of bodies, but it was said that about four thousand perished. They were shot one or two kilometers from the sawmill, near the sandy pits that were situated by the Green Bridge. We were working at the sawmill and we heard the cracks of the machine-gun fire.

When the day passed, stillness crept in and we returned to the ghetto. We witnessed the great destruction: this one had no wife, this one had no child and this one had no brother. Abnormality set in, but we had to adjust and live within the given conditions in a so-called normal fashion. Again, we began a life of ghetto normality.

Until the day of destruction, Jews would walk individually. After the slaughter, the rule was to walk in groups, with a leader of that group.

I was one of the individuals that decided to become part of the ghetto underground. I believe that it was one of the first organizations that were established to revolt against the Germans. I belonged to the First Fifth. I was introduced by Hatski, the locksmith, who knew me well. With his recommendation, I was taken into the group.

Why did I belong to the First Fifth? My house, by Yosel the carpenter, was the second from the ghetto gate. From there, began the count. At the risk of our lives we recovered weapons. We had different strategies: either to flee into the forest and /or to begin the revolt.

It turned out that the German spies hadn't been sleeping. They smelled that something was going on in the ghetto. One nice day, when going to work in groups, we were encircled. We were brought to the department of the commissariat. The building had once been a bank. They encircled us. One of the German leaders appeared, as well as a Jewish leader. He was the leader after Isakson, who had been murdered during the first *Aktion*. He was one of the grandest personalities of Baranovich. They told us that we would be brought to work. They chose one thousand men, one by one – men who were young and also older men who were healthy and strong.

They brought us by train in closed cabins, to the yard of Molodechno From there we were taken to the New and Old Vilayke. In Vilayke, we were separated into groups. One group had seven hundred men and the second group had three hundred men. I was placed in the group of three hundred men.

Later on it became known that the group of seven hundred men existed for six to eight weeks. They were exposed to a typhus epidemic. A portion died of typhus and the remainder were killed.

Our camp was administered by a Jew whose name was Avraham Mazurek. He had been a lawyer in Warsaw. We chose him as camp leader. Our work consisted of laying rails on the road that went to Vitebsk. There was only one line, but the Germans wanted to build another one. This was our job.

At the time that we were to conclude the job, we had a premonition that something would occur in Baranovich, or that it was in the process of happening. It was the New Year of 1943. We did not know it then, but the Baranovich ghetto was being liquidated. I turned to Mazurek and proposed that we all escape to the forest. Avraham Mazurek, the camp leader, responded, "I will give the order when to escape to the forest."

I opposed him. I organized about fifty people who wanted to enter the forest. But Avraham Mazurek was the camp leader, so people feared him. We chose to wait until more people joined us before escaping.

Where was the forest located?

The forest was located sixteen kilometers from Old Vilayke, from the shtetl of Kurenets. Mazurek was connected with a group from the shtetl Oshmyany, and disappeared with them in the forest. He left the camp without leadership. He knew that from the camp we would be transported to another place. In truth, he made an agreement with the German leader, Kelerman. Kelerman was more of a salesman than a Nazi. He was duly rewarded for his attitude.

Our camp was transported to Bezdani, which was close to Vilna. I called the place Biz Danen [Yiddish for "up to here"].

After Mazurek fled, Brod was selected as leader. He was a medical student in Warsaw. He was married to the sister of Aharon Slutski, who was the editor of the *Baranovisher Tsaytung*. Brod behaved in the same manner as Mazurek. "We cannot escape into the forest," he declared, "since we have with us 20 old Jews." I responded that to save 280, we must give up 20. He did not accept my opinion.

In the new camp, we dug peat. The Germans needed the peat as Jews needed pain! This is what the Germans wanted and to try to understand them!

On one nice day, June 13, the camp was encircled. Weiss and Kitell came to say that the workers should be brought to camp. There were two hundred workers. At all times, there were at least one hundred men present in camp. When the men arrived, the camp was not as yet surrounded by soldiers. They were hiding in the forest (the camp was located in the middle of a forest).

I was one of the first to realize that the end was near, so I fled. Other people followed me. Six men saved themselves. I remember some of them. There was a boy from Baranovich but I have forgotten his name. I decided that we should travel to Vilna, because I thought there were still Jews in the Vilna Ghetto.

When we came to New Vileyka, I went to a young Jewish man named Isrolek Roshinishak. He was a colony leader of the Vilna workers who were assigned to the train station. They accompanied me to the Vilna Ghetto. Upon entering the Vilna Ghetto, Byalostatskin and I were arrested for not wearing the special Vilna Ghetto tags that were worn by the ghetto people. We were arrested by Solomon Gens, the police inspector, Sgt. Shmulevitsh and Levos, the commander of the ghetto yard. Shmuelevitsh and Gens were sympathetic individuals, but on Levos' face I saw a murderous glare.

After three days of being held captive, we were freed. We were not considered prisoners but we were held because of security. They wanted to know who we were.

While in the ghetto, I became acquainted with a young man whose name was Joseph Harmatz. I mournfully said to him, "I have nothing to lose. If we revolt in the ghetto, I will join you." My plan was to go into the forest. He smiled and said, "In the morning, I will give you an answer." The next morning he came back with an answer: "She said that you belong to us." "She" was Khyene

Borowska, who was the political commissar of the underground movement of the Vilna ghetto. I obeyed all of the orders that were given to me. I was ready to fight in the streets of the Vilna ghetto. On September 23, when the last group of fighters of the United Partisan Organization crawled through the sewers to reach the forest, I was with them. The leader of the group was Joseph Harmatz, from the Fifth Part. The general leadership was under Aba Kovner, who took over the leadership from Isaac Wittenberg after Wittenberg died a terrible death.

Shmuel Kaplinski was assigned by the staff as commander of the Second Detachment and Khyene Borowska as the political commissar of the partisans. They assigned me as Shmuel Kaplinski's representative. I was his representative until I was assigned as commander of the Third Detachment. Our cry was "Death to the Fascist." One of our leaders was Captain Vaselnitski, who did not want to be identified as a Jew but was, in fact, a Jew. He had escaped from the Ninth Unit in Kovno. Another leader was a certain old Communist, who had come from another forest after having been expelled from Moscow. They came into the forest and were assigned as commanders of the Third and Fourth Detachments. They proposed that I would become chief of staff. I refused, preferring to return to my detachment.

Upon returning to the Second Detachment, I encountered confusion about which I will not give any details at this time. Shmuel Kaplinski, Khyene Borowska and Aba Kovner were admonished by the brigade staff. In fact, the staff consisted of only one man, named Gavris. He was a Lithuanian who was married to a Jewess. After the war he went on to become an influential judge in Lithuania. In any case, Gavris assigned me as the commander of the Second Detachment.

Please tell me about the development of the detachment. Why was the detachment created? What type of individuals joined the detachment? Where did they come from? How was ammunition procured? What military actions occurred? What was the relationship with the Russian partisans?

The Jews that arrived in the forest were the remnants of the unfortunate Vilna ghetto. We were labeled as part of the partisans' Lithuanian Brigade. The Jews composed the majority of the people who populated the Rudnicki Forest.

There were also Russian groups. They were so-called military specialists, but in fact they were unable to outclass us. We were young men and women of the Vilna Ghetto, who had never heard gunshots in our lives! Even with such a background, we were able to achieve a level of first-class excellence. I was a military man. I had gone to training school. A gun was not a stranger to me, nor were automatics or canons. I knew the trade. I was amazed at the courage of my fellow partisans. In time, they learned to go out and fearlessly scout the terrain, plant mines and cut telephone wires.

We operated within our environment and the given opportunities. Our operations were limited. There were times when German trains were running day and night and we couldn't do anything because we did not have the equipment to blow them up. There were other times when we did have the explosives that were parachuted to us and we were able to stop the flow of the German transportation system. The Germans were afraid to travel by day and of course the fear was more evident at night. I myself blew up three train lines: two going between Kovno and Vilna and one from Lida to Vilna.

The toughest operations were to obtain food supplies. There were hundreds of us, and we all needed to eat. The food was obtained from far-off villages that were armed by the Germans.

We lost many men and women under different circumstances: laying mines, crossing rivers and other dangerous and unfortunate occurrences. Though we were only from the ghetto, I believe that we excelled in our duties on par with those who were Moscow-trained. We Jewish partisans would work together with the Russian partisans on missions. There were times when the Russian partisans would become drunk, leaving the horse-drawn wagons containing mines standing idly by the houses. We did not make an issue of it, but went about our business to complete our mission.

I believe that the Jewish partisans of the Lithuanian Brigade, and especially those of the Rudnicki Forest, were outstanding fighters. The leader, Pulkovnik Gavris, was a liberal, a nice person, highly esteemed by his men.

Is it correct that there were four detachments active in the Rudnicki Forest?

Yes! The names of the commanders of these detachments, myself excluded, were Shmuel Kaplinski, Aba Kovner (at the beginning), Hanan Magid and

Imke Loybatski. The other detachments had other commanders. The active and factual leaders were the ones that I named.

Were the detachments completely Jewish?

In my detachment, there were 120 people. Of those, there were four Lithuanians, one Pole, one Dutch, ten Russians and the rest were Jews. The detachment was then split into platoons, and the platoon into smaller groups.

My assistant was Joseph Harmtaz. The battalion commander was Mitie Lifnhalts. The leader for gathering information was Yitzhak Tshuzshy. The remaining members were an excellent group, able to operate even without commanders. Tuvya Rubin was the chief; he ensured that food would be available.

What was the division of men and women?

I think that there were seventy-five men and thirty-five women.

What was the percentage of P.A.P. members?

I really do not know; I think 30 percent of the women.

What do you know about the actions of Yehiel Shaynboym in your area in the Rudnicki Forest?

Their excellence related to the fact that they were called Yehiel Shaynboym's group. In truth, they were just a partisan unit like any other group. Maybe they felt within themselves, that they were special. In fact, they were one group of many that followed orders of the leaders.

What was the procedure for accepting a new recruit? Were their definite rules? Were there limitations?

It is difficult for me to answer this. In the time of Shmuel Kaplinski, Aba Kovner and Khyene Borowska, they would only accept new members who possessed ammunition. I did not like that. These was difficult times, but they should not have disqualified anyone. There were times that men and women, or women and children, stood at a distance. They would not allow them into the camp. With great courage on my part, I convinced the leaders to let them come in. A woman named Reznik can bear witness. She lives in Israel. A woman named Gordon, with two boys, can also give witness. It was a sad truth, but the truth.

What was the relationship between the Jewish and non-Jewish partisans? What was your relationship with the Soviet commander?

It is my feeling that anti-Semitism did not play any role. It was not the time or the place. They had ammunition and we had ammunition.

Did the Soviet commander plan your movements in the Rudnicki Forest?

Plans of action were administered by each commander. There were not any coordinated actions. I would turn to the leaders and ask them why actions weren't coordinated. They answered that it was easier this way. Later, I came to agree with them. An operation of greater magnitude would result in greater casualties. Smaller groups incurred fewer casualties while still obtaining objectives.

Were there casualties from your detachment?

Absolutely. I went on a lot of missions. I was no hero, but I did have a lot of luck! When I went south the Germans went north. When we made contact, I lost about twelve soldiers from the detachment. This was all that I lost. Some of the people killed were Loybatski, Danke, Lole Frukhna, Rashl Markovitsh, Manyek Radzyevitsh, Avraham Rabinovitch and Motl Gopstein. I will list the rest of the names in a letter; I have a record of all of the names.

How many Jews were shot or were lost in the forest? What were the causes? How did the partisans react to crisis situations? We know that Khyene Borowska ordered some partisans shot!

When we came into the forest, the agreement among the partisans was to attack. We did not know who set the tempo, or who the leaders were. There was anger. At that time, the commissar of the brigade was a man by the name of Zimanas, or Ziman in Yiddish. His name in the forest was Yurgis. He had been thrown off the staff of the Lithuanian Partisan Movement that was centered in Moscow. Zimanas's deputy of personnel and political matters was Stankavitsh. He was an old and hardened Communist. A great portion of his life had been lived in prison. He was true to his beliefs. I don't know the facts, but some policemen who came into the forest were accused of collaborating with the Germans. I do not believe it. They wore the uniform of the Jewish Police; they were never involved in any murders. They never had an opportunity to murder, nor did they have the talent for it. Maybe they gave a slap. They were made the scapegoats by leaders of the brigade, who ordered that they be taken out and shot.

I will admit that when the murders occurred, I lost all confidence in the leadership. It was an ugly way of handling the situation. I could not agree with it. No partisan could have agreed with such an action.

Being organized in the Rudnicki Forest, did you have a central base or did you travel from place to place?
What were your operational possibilities?

The Rudnicki Forest was one of the best forests. It had a number of positives and one negative. The negative was that the train line from Lida to Vilna ran through the forest. The Germans would travel this route to ensure the safety of the route. Therefore, there were a few German garrisons present. The positive aspects were that it was dense, muddy and hard, which was excellent for planning maneuvers. Another positive: we were able to bring food from the west, north and south. Also, there were opportunities to perform operations, plant mines and cut telegraph and phone wires. It was a fitting place for military activities.

We were tremendously lucky that the war speeded it up and we were quickly freed. If not, the Germans would have destroyed us.

One time I attacked two German trucks containing German soldiers. I had forty men at my disposal. In seconds, the Germans were killed. We captured their ammunition, and turned over the trucks. We left their corpses on the causeway. In the afternoon, German tanks came to remove the corpses. We took their captured automatic guns and grenades. It was some operation. In May of 1944, not far from Vishintsi Bridge, one kilometer from there, a German garrison was in place. We destroyed them without the Germans firing a shot.

Did you have contacts in the ghetto before the liquidation of the Vilna Ghetto? What was the relationship like between the ghetto underground and the partisans?

I was not familiar with the situation. I belonged to the staff and did not know any of the contacts. I believe the contacts were at a minimum. They sent partisans to the Narocz Forest. It was a distance of 200 kilometers, when the Rudnicki Forest was 15 kilometers.

I believe that I should not criticize, since I wasn't there the entire time. But it would have been possible to transfer more Jews to the Rudnicki Forest.

What were your relations with the Soviet regiments who were in the forest?

There were a few Soviet regiments, with their commanders and specialists from Russia. They had their responsibilities, as Kontra-Razvedka. They worked in conjunction with the General Staff. They did their work and we did ours. They did not bother us and we did not bother them. There was never an instance of their attacking Jewish partisans. We did not feel any bad blood. When I hear of actions in other forests, as by the Beilski partisans, or others, I am amazed. By us, there was no such thing, and I do not know of other such activities.

Can you describe the meeting of the Red Army?

When we left the forest, we encountered a group. From a distance, we did not know who they were. Then we found out that they were White Poles, who operated in the villages and not in the forests. They were hidden and from time to time they came out of hiding and attacked us. We frequently engaged with them; they killed many partisans. When we met, we greeted each other with a white flag. We exchanged positions: they entered the forest and we left the forest.

When we neared Vilna, we encountered Soviet tanks manned by Jewish Russian soldiers. They were happy to be meeting up with Jewish partisans.

This was on July 14, 1944. We arrived in Vilna and participated in street battles. The Jewish partisans showed the Russians how to fight and how to cross the river.

In Vilna, there was a strong German regiment. Soon individuals were arrested. Hundreds of bodies were lying in the street. They were shot. We took it upon ourselves to watch the bridges, the important buildings and the warehouses.

On the third day a Jewish-Soviet war correspondent arrived – Ilya Ehrenburg. We took pictures with him. He seemed happy to encounter a large group of Jewish partisans.

What was his first reaction?

The first reaction was one of friendship. I felt joy. His face was full of smiles. He had great pleasure being with us, and he asked us about our activities. He wanted to know what we had accomplished. He wrote everything down and then publicized our exploits.

They took movies of us. Both male and female partisans spoke into microphones. Afterwards, the films were shown in Russia. I saw pictures of us in Soviet newspapers.

After being together for a few weeks, we abandoned the regiments. The partisans were able to find work in the city, in different offices. Some joined the militia. In a short time the well-known flight to the West began. It was carried on in secret.

I had a post working for the train company. I was a member of the food-supply business that supplied the train workers. I worked for a year and a half, up until May of 1946.

Did you receive distinctions?

Every partisan received a medal. The medal's inscription read: "Partisan First Class." Another medal was for the victory for the fatherland. There were also partisans who received war commendations: "The Red Star," or Krasnaye Zvezda. These were medals of a higher order. I was to receive these awards, but time did not allow it. The partisans left from Lithuania for the west.

After the liberation, was there a Zionist effort to transport Jews to Israel?

After the liberation, while still in Vilna, I looked at Vilna as a transient city. I belonged and yet I did not belong. I knew hundreds of Jews, both partisans and regular Jews. I knew people traveling to Poland or further towards the West. Outwardly, Jews did not express any special inclinations towards Israel. If there was such a feeling, it was kept very private because of fear of a conspiracy.

I knew a lot of groups that decided to travel there. I myself wanted to go, but later we couldn't operate openly, and I don't know what happened.

I exercised my right as a Polish citizen and returned to Seltz. It was my birthplace. From there, I gathered all of my documents and left Poland to go to Germany. In Germany I was a businessman, like other Jews. I did not become rich. I was ready to travel to Israel but since my mother was raised in America and she had a large family there, I came to America.

Today, I visited Israel for the first time.

When did you marry? What is the name of your wife?

Her name is Luba Weiskopf. She came from Tamashov Mazavyetski. She lived in Vilna. She was with the partisans. We have three sons. Two are married and the third is seventeen years old.

Notes

Chapter 1

1. Author unknown, "Polish Theatre Blitzkrieg," *Time Magazine*, September 25, 1939, accessed February 10, 2015.

2. Yehuda Vilechik, "The Loss of our Parents and Dear Sisters and Brothers," *Kartuz-Bereza, Our Town Memorial Book*, p. 187, accessed February 10, 2015, http://www.jewishgen.org/yizkor/bereza93/ber179.html#Page187.

3. Steven J. Zalog, *Poland 1939: The Birth of Blitzkrieg* (Oxford: Osprey Publishing, 2002), pp. 9–12.

4. Martin Gilbert, *Atlas of the Holocaust* (New York: William Morrow & Co., 1993), map 3 for Brest-Litovsk, maps 33–34 for the Bug River as frontier between Russia and Germany beginning in September 1939.

5. Gilbert, *Atlas of the Holocaust*, maps 33–34; Rivne (Rowne).

6. Archibald L. Patterson, *Between Hitler and Stalin: The Quick Life and Secret Death of Edward Smigly Rydz, Marshal of Poland* (Indianapolis, IN: Dog Ear Publishing, 2010), pp. 174–75, 177, 228–29.

7. Gilbert, *Atlas of the Holocaust*, Maps 33–34 for the Bug River as frontier between Russia and Germany beginning in September 1939.

8. Moishe Tuchman, "The Destruction of Kartuz," *Kartuz-Bereza: Our Town Memorial Book*, ed. Chaim Ben Israel, Organization of Survivors of Kartuz-Bereza (Tel Aviv, 1993), accessed October 30, 2013, http://www.jewishgen.org/yizkor/bereza93/bereza93.html#TOC.

9. Author unknown, "Seltz," in *Memorial Book of Five Destroyed Communities: Pruzhany, Belarus* (*Pinkas me-hamesh kehilot harevot*), ed. Mordechai W. Bernstein (Buenos Aires, 1958) accessed October 30, 2013, http://www.jewishgen.org/Yizkor/Pruzhany/pru557.html.

   David Beckler, "On the Jews of Selcz, Kartuz Bereza and Their Sad End," *Kartuz-Bereza, Our Town Memorial Book*, ed. Chaim Ben Israel, Organization of Survivors of Kartuz-Breza (Tel Aviv, 1993), accessed February 10, 2015, http://www.jewishgen.org/yizkor/bereza93/ber179.html#Page190.

10. Herman Kruk, "The Frightful Tragedy of the Baranovich Jews," *The Baranovich Memorial Book* (Tel Aviv, 1953), pp. 8–9; printed in *Baranovich in Martyrdom and Resistance*, comp. and ed. Joseph Foxman (New York: Baranovich Society of America, 1964), part 2 of the trilogy *Sefer zikaron Baranovich* [Memorial book of Baronovich] (Mahwah, NJ: Jacob. S. Berger, 2012).

11. Motl Machtai, "Steibtz of the Past," *Memorial Volume of Steibtz-Swerznie and the Neighboring Villages Rubezhevitz, Derevna, Nalibok* (*Stowbtsy, Belarus*), ed. Nachum Hinitz, trans. Esther Libby Raichman, accessed October 30, 2013, http://www.jewishgen.org/yizkor/Stowbtsy/sto191.html; Getzel Reiser, "In the Ghetto and in the Concentration Camp," ibid., http://www.jewishgen.org/yizkor/Stowbtsy/sto316.html, accessed April 2, 2015.

12. Gilbert, *Atlas of the Holocaust*, map 73, Baranovich (Baranowicze).

13. Zelik Levinbook, "The Destruction of Baranovich Jewry," in *The Baranovich Memorial Book* (Tel Aviv, 1953), part 1 of the trilogy *Sefer zikaron Baranovich*, p. 475.

Chapter 2

1. Shmuel Yankelewicz, "On the Ruins," *The Baranovich Memorial Book* (Tel Aviv, 1953), part 1 of the trilogy *Sefer zikaron Baranovich*, pp. 373–78.

2. Eliezer Lidowsky, "The Resistance Organization," in *The Baranovich Memorial Book* (Tel Aviv, 1953), part 1 of the trilogy *Sefer zikaron Baranovich*, p. 351.

3. Ibid.

4. Pinchas Mordkowsky, "We Flee the Koldichevo Camp to the Partisans," in *Baranovich in Martyrdom and Resistance*, part 2 of the trilogy *Sefer zikaron Baranovich*, pp. 5–7.

5. Gilbert, *Atlas of the Holocaust*; see page 83 for a brief history of the vans and map 127.

6. Yankelewicz, "On the Ruins," pp. 373–78.

7. Levinbook, "The Destruction of Baranovich Jewry," pp. 420–21.

8. Lidowsky, "The Resistance Organization," p. 350.

9. Joseph Foxman, *In the Shadow of Death* (Jerusalem: Yad Vashem and the Holocaust Survivors' Memoirs Project, 2011).

10. Levinbook, "The Destruction of Baranovich Jewry," p. 396.

11. Ibid., pp. 394–400.

12. Dinah Porat, in *The Fall of a Sparrow* (Stanford, CA: Stanford University Press, 2010), p. 44, describes *Aktionen* (plural of *Aktion*) as "the systematic raids to round up the Jewish population."

13. Levinbook, "The Destruction of Baranovich Jewry," p. 410.

14. Ibid., pp. 408–9.

15. Ibid., p. 411.

16. Moshe Mukasey, "Between Both World Wars 1919–39," in *The Baranovich Memorial Book*, part 1 of the trilogy *Sefer zikaron Baranovich*, pp. 74–92.

17. Yankelewicz, "On the Ruins," pp. 373–78.

Chapter 3

1. Eliezer Lidowsky, "The Resistance Organization," in *The Baranovich Memorial Book*, part 1 of the trilogy *Sefer zikaron Baranovich*, p. 369.

2. Ibid., p. 352.

3. Ibid., p. 440.

4. Ibid., p. 352.

5. Ibid.

6. Kruk, "The Frightful Tragedy of the Baranovich Jews," p. 9.

7. Robert S. Wistrich, *Who's Who in Nazi Germany* (New York: Routledge, 2001), pp. 259–60.

8. Lidowsky, "The Resistance Organization," p. 440.

9. Ibid., p. 369.

10. Ibid., p. 367.

11. Baruch Kudewicky, "Uprising in the Old-Wilejka Camp," *Baranovich in Martyrdom and Resistance*, part 2 of the trilogy *Sefer zikaron Baranovich*, pp. 17–20.

12. Meir Elin, "The Death Forts of Kovno," *The Complete Black Book of Russian Jewry*, eds. Ilya Ehrenburg and Vasily Grossman, trans. David Patterson (New Brunswick, NJ: Transaction Publishers, 2011), p. 323.

Chapter 4

1. Sh. Klass, "An Overview of the City," *The Struggle to Stay Alive*, eds. Yitzhak Posner and Chana Bint (Tel Aviv: Arieli Press, 1992), part 3 of the trilogy *Sefer zikaron Baranovich*, p. v.

2. Abba Kovner, *The Scrolls of Testimony*, trans. Eddie Levenston (Philadelphia: Jewish Publication Society, 2001).

3. Kudewicky, "Uprising in the Old-Wilejka Camp," pp. 17–20.

4. Levinbook, "The Destruction of Baranovich Jewry," p. 475.

5. Yitzhak Arad, *Ghetto in Flames* (New York: Holocaust Library, 1982), p. 335.

6. Levinbook, "The Destruction of Baranovich Jewry," p. 436.

7. Rachel Margolis, introduction to *Ponary Diary* by Kazimierz Sakowicz, ed. Yitzhak Arad (New Haven: Yale University Press, 1999), p. vii.

8. Arad, *Ghetto in Flames*, p. 368.

9. Ibid., p. 369.

10. Avrom Sutskever, "The Vilna Ghetto," trans. M. Shambadal and B. Chernyak, in *The Complete Black Book of Russian Jewry*, pp. 251–53.

11. Arad, *Ghetto in Flames*, p. 243.

Chapter 5

1. Isaac Kowalski, *A Secret Press in Nazi Europe* (New York: Shengold Publishers, 1969), p. 60.

2. N.N. Shneidman, *The Three Tragic Heroes of the Vilnius Ghetto* (New York: Mosaic Press, 2002), pp. 120–21.

3. Arad, *Ghetto in Flames*, p. 427.

4. Ibid., p. 470.

5. Joseph Harmatz, *From the Wings* (Hove, UK: The Book Guild, 1998), p. 77.

6. Arad, *Ghetto in Flames*, 1982, p. 425.

7. Kowalski, *A Secret Press in Nazi Europe*, p. 214.

8. Ibid., p. 51.

9. Ibid., p. 96.

10. Foxman, *In the Shadow of Death*, p. 47n.

11. Kowalski, *A Secret Press in Nazi Europe*, p. 215.

12. Harmatz, *From the Wings*, pp. 74, 75–76, 139–41.

13. Arad, *Ghetto in Flames*, pp. 189, 190n.; Rich Cohen, *The Avengers* (New York: Vintage Books, 2000).

14. "Chaim Mordechai Rumkowski," Holocaust Education and Archive Research Team, accessed November 5, 2013, http://www.holocaustresearchproject.org/ghettos/rumkowski.html.

15. Kowalski, *A Secret Press in Nazi Europe*, p. 58. For a general description of the FPO, see "United Partisan Organization, Vilna," Shoah Resource Center, The International School for Holocaust Studies, accessed November 5, 2013, http://www1.yadvashem.org/odot_pdf/Microsoft%20Word%20-%205902.pdf.

16. Kowalski, *A Secret Press in Nazi Europe*, pp. 115, 220.

17. Porat, *The Fall of a Sparrow*.

18. Cohen, *The Avengers*, p. 109.

19. The so-called "Wittenberg Affair" puts the dilemma into sharp focus; see Porat, *The Fall of a Sparrow*, pp. 106–31; see also Kowalski, *A Secret Press in Nazi Europe*, pp. 139–44; Arad, *Ghetto in Flames*, pp. 387–95.

20. Ibid.

21. Kowalski, *A Secret Press in Nazi Europe*, p. 214; see also Porat, *The Fall of a Sparrow*, p. 144.

22. Masha Greenbaum, *The Jews of Lithuania: A History of a Remarkable Community, 1316–1945* (Jerusalem: Gefen, 1995), p. 304.

23. Arad, *Ghetto in Flames*, pp. 396–98; on Yurgis's order, see ibid., p. 424.

24. Shneidman, *The Three Tragic Heroes of the Vilnius Ghetto*, p. 106.

25. Ibid., pp. 120–21.

26. Kowalski, *A Secret Press in Nazi Europe*, pp. 134–40.

27. Shneidman, *The Three Tragic Heroes of the Vilnius Ghetto*. p. 111.

28. Arad, *Ghetto in Flames*, pp. 360–64.

Chapter 6

1. Joseph Harmatz, "Leaving the Ghetto for the Woods," *Jewish Resistance in the Holocaust*, accessed November 7, 2013, http://c3.ort.org.il/Apps/WW/page.aspx?ws=496fe4b2-4d9a-4c28-a845-510b28b1e44b&page=5d675d48-68df-4fc3-833c-04a23648f70e&fol=e5b35888-e7db-4e50-9ce4-e132ae92de2e&box=3e0902e0-b315-412c-a5ec-927e5dab4302&_pstate=item&_item=d1caf6df-4723-40dc-bfcd-c72f988b6f23.

2. Balberyszski, *Stronger Than Iron*, pp. 245–79.

3. Cohen, *The Avengers*, p. 97; see also Porat, *The Fall of a Sparrow*, p. 145; Harmatz, *From the Wings*, pp. 36–37.

4. Harmatz, "Leaving the Ghetto for the Woods."

5. Kowalski, *A Secret Press in Nazi Europe*, p. 220.

6. Harmatz, "Leaving the Ghetto for the Woods."

7. Arad, *Ghetto in Flames*, p. 368.

8. Nechama Tec, *Defiance* (New York: Oxford University Press, 1993), p. 131.

9. Sutskever, "The Vilna Ghetto," p. 291.

Chapter 7

1. Dimitri Ghelpernus, "In the Ghetto Grip," *Kovno Ghetto Diary*, trans. Chaim Bargman, accessed February 18, 2015, http://www.jewishgen.org/yizkor/kaunas/Kaunas.html#TOC.

2. David M. Glantz, foreword to *The Partisans Companion: Updated and Revised 1942*, eds. Lester Grau and Michael Gress (Philadelphia: Casemate Publishers, 2011); Arad, *Ghetto in Flames*, pp. 247–62.

3. Yitzhak Arad, *In the Shadow of the Red Banner* (Jerusalem: Gefen, 2010), p. 289.

4. Kowalski, *A Secret Press in Nazi Europe*, p. 238.

5. Yitzhak Arad, *The Partisan* (New York: Holocaust Library, 1979), p. 149.

6. Arad, *The Partisan*, p. 160. See also Harry J. Cargas, "An Interview with Yitzhak Arad," *Voices from the Holocaust* (University Press of Kentucky, 1993), accessed April 3 2015, http://kehilalinks. jewishgen.org/Svencionys/interview_with_arad.html.

7. Arad, *Ghetto in Flames*, p. 458.

8. Lester Grau and Michael Gress, eds., *The Partisans Companion: Updated and Revised 1942* (Philadelphia: Casemate Publishers, 2011), p. 212.

9. Arad, *Ghetto in Flames*, p. 451.

10. "Vilna During the Holocaust," in *The Story of the Jewish Community of Vilna*, accessed October 8, 2013, http://www.yadvashem.org/yv/en/exhibitions/vilna/during/partisans_rudniki_forest.asp.

11. Leon Berk, *Destined to Live* (Melbourne, Australia: Paragon Press, 1992); Kowalski, *A Secret Press in Nazi Europe*, p. 285.

12. For information regarding Rushka Korzak's arrival in Palestine, see Cohen, *The Avengers*, pp. 170–71; see also Neima Barzel, "Rozka Korczak-Marla," in *Jewish Women: A Comprehensive Historical Encyclopedia*, accessed October 8, 2013, http://jwa.org/encyclopedia/article/korczak-marla-rozka.

Chapter 8

1. Arad, *Ghetto in Flames*, p. 458. For a description of the Beilski camp, see Tec, *Defiance*, chapter 11.

2. Arad, *In the Shadow of the Red Banner*, p. 284.

3. Harmatz, *From the Wings*, pp. 84–85.

4. Kowalski, *A Secret Press in Nazi Europe*, pp. 242–43.

5. "Khutor Farming," in *The Great Soviet Encyclopedia*, 3rd ed. (The Gale Group, 1970–1979), accessed February 18, 2015, http://encyclopedia2.thefreedictionary.com/Khutor+Farming.

6. Viktor Suvorov, *Spetsnaz* (London: Grafton Books, 1989), pp. 13–17.

7. Chaim Lazar, *Destruction and Uprising*, pp. 328–33, Yad Vashem.org. "Vilna during the Holocaust," accessed October 11, 2013, http://www.yadvashem.org/yv/en/exhibitions/vilna/during/partisans_rudniki_forest.asp.

8. Elin, "The Death Forts of Kovno," p. 314.

9. Ibid., p. 322.

10. Kowalski, *A Secret Press in Nazi Europe*, p. 221.

11. Ibid., pp. 70,142. Arad, *Ghetto in Flames*, p. 456, n. 15; see also Kowalski, *A Secret Press in Nazi Europe*, p. 241.

12. Arad, *In the Shadow of the Red Banner*, p. 285.

13. Sutskever, "The Vilna Ghetto," p. 291.

14. Harmatz, *From the Wings*, p. 90.

15. Porat, *The Fall of a Sparrow*, p. 166

16. Harmatz, *From the Wings*, pp. 153–54; Porat, *The Fall of a Sparrow*, pp. 166, 169.

Chapter 9

1. Harmatz, *From the Wings*, p. 87.

2. Tome Barton, "Samogon," *Russiapedia*, accessed October 12, 2013, http://russiapedia.rt.com/of-russian-origin/samogon/.

3. Harmatz, *From the Wings*, p. 88.

4. "Chaim Yellin," *The Virtual Shtetl Project*, accessed October 13, 2013. http://www.shtetl.lt/m/en/people/252/

5. Arad, *In the Shadow of the Red Banner*, p. 283.

6. "Olkieniki," *The Untold Stories*, Yadvashem.org., accessed October 13, 2013. http://www.yadvashem.org/untoldstories/database/index.asp?cid=187.

7. Kowalski, *A Secret Press in Nazi Europe*, p. 279.

Chapter 10

1. "Ilya Ehrenburg," Wikipedia, accessed October 13, 2013, http://en.wikipedia.org/wiki/Ilya_Ehrenburg#cite_note-3. See also Ilya Ehrenburg, "Kill," accessed February 19, 2015, http://militera.lib.ru/prose/russian/erenburg_ig3/091.html.

2. Porat, *The Fall of a Sparrow*, pp. 172–73.

3. Aleksandr Tvardovsky, "Tribute to Ilya Ehrenburg," SOVLIT.net., accessed February 19, 2015, http://www.sovlit.net/ehrenburgtribute/; see also "Ehrenburg, Ilya Grigorvich," *Encyclopedia of Soviet Writers*, SOVLIT.net., accessed February 19, 2015, http://www.sovlit.net/bios/ehrenburg.html; "Ilya Ehrenburg," Wikipedia, accessed October 13, 2013, http://en.wikipedia.org/wiki/Ilya_Ehrenburg#cite_note-3.

4. Ibid.; see also Ilya Ehrenburg, "Kill."

5. Ruth R. Wisse, "Sutzkever, Avrom," *The Yivo Encyclopedia of Jews in Eastern Europe*, accessed February 19, 2015, http://www.yivoencyclopedia.org/article.aspx/Sutzkever_Avrom.

6. "Konigsberg," Wikipedia, accessed February 19, 2015, http://en.wikipedia.org/wiki/K%C3%B6nigsberg.